Embracing Divine Grace

Embracing Divine Grace

A Life Story of a Man
From Transylvania, Romania

By John Hunyady

Order this book online at www.trafford.com
or email orders@trafford.com

Most Trafford titles are also available at major online book retailers.

Printed in the United States of America.

ISBN: 978-1-4269-9299-5 (sc)
ISBN: 978-1-4269-9300-8 (e)

Trafford rev. 10/26/2011

 www.trafford.com

North America & international
toll-free: 1 888 232 4444 (USA & Canada)
phone: 250 383 6864 ♦ fax: 812 355 4082

My name is John Hunyady. Although Hunyady is a Hungarian name, I am Hungarian only by name; I am of German descent. I was born at home with the help of a midwife on May 20, 1926, to a Lutheran family in the village of Heidendorf in Transylvania, Romania. My village was founded by many German settlers. New settlers had come into the village through the years. They fought their foes for centuries. They fought for their land. Their foes were the Romans and the Turks, and at one time, the heathen occupied this land. The German settlers fought them off. The later settlers were Lutherans, as we were in 1944. In English, the name of the village is Heiden Village.

The village where I was born.

In 1441, King Geiza had just come to the throne. He decided to call people to immigrate to our part of the world. They settled to the south of Transylvania to the Black Sea. I learned in school that the German settlers came from everywhere. They were all farmers and needed a lot of land to farm, so they settled to the Carpathian Mountains. They fought many bloody battles with the Romans and Turks. The Saxons had come into a society with dysfunctional marital unity. People sold their children and killed the ones that were not sold. As a result, hunger, pestilence,

1

and death broke out. In time, a new leader came in. His name was John Hunyady. During those early years, he led a Christian army and fought off the Turks. He went along the Danube River. (Hundreds of years later, another John Hunyady was at the same river, and that was me.) He came with a request for all people to live in marital unity. By that time, the immigrants called this part of the land Transylvania. They proclaimed that the people were Transylvania Saxons, and that is how it still was in 1944.

There were still many battles between the Saxons and the Turks. Their prisoners were sent home with their noses and ears cut off. Their German women were raped, their children killed by the Tartans. There was nobody available to harvest their crops. That happened twice, one time each year. I perceive that my village underwent many heartaches. They lost their homes through fires started by smoking. Farmers and workers were out in the field. When they came home, they found their village had burned out. They had nowhere to go. They dug holes in the hills for shelter from the rain.

There was a man in our village by the name of Ruhrig. (I knew the family name quite well.) He had the largest winery in the village. He sold most of his wine to rebuild the village. They were so happy that the village was near a large forest. They could use that lumber to rebuild their houses. They had no church or school at that time. I read in the history books that all the documentation of the village was lost in that fire. There were also hard times for farming the land because of extremely dry conditions.

In 1873, the farmers sowed their seed on their land. Everything looked good weather wise. By June, the whole area was gasping for rain, fog, or dew. The trees that bloomed were so nice. Soon the corn and pumpkins were all gone. Nothing grew.

When people emigrated from Luxembourg, Germany, they lived on farms. The grandfathers were born there and died there. They did not have old age homes; families looked after their own. When the oldest son got married, his wife brought with her a dowry, which provided for more work and production. In 1979, I went to Luxembourg. There, the people spoke the same German dialect as I did.

My father said to me, "Many years ago a Hungarian man came to Transylvania and met a German lady, and the rest is history." My father and mother were born in Bistritz (a city 5 kilometers to the east) and later settled in Heidendorf village. The village was looking for a miller, so they hired my dad. I had three older sisters, Maria, Sophie, and Rose, who were also born at Bistritz, and one brother Michael, who was two years younger than me. I never met my grandparents.

My sisters Sophie and Rose and my brother Michael and I.

My mom Maria and my dad John. He was an officer in the Hungarian Army in WW I.

In my village my dad managed the village mill. We had other men working for us as laborers by the week or month. In 1925, with the help of the people from our village, my dad installed electricity in the mill and town. The men dug holes for lampposts, and Dad strung two wires up, one line after the other, with one bulb for each house and streetlight. When strong winds blew, the electrical wires would tangle up. From that point on, no one had electricity. Someone would come and tell us. When I was older, it was usually my job to untangle the wires. I had two long poles, and another man and I would pull the wires apart.

I remember that at home, I had seen prison inmates out to build roads. I had seen wagons full of heavy rocks dumped. The prisoners had sledge hammers, and they started to chip away at that rock. Then the rocks would be made smaller and smaller until small enough to be used in road building. I got to know the warden through my dad.

We only had dirt roads, which were good as long as it did not rain much. When it rained, heavily loaded wagons would sink up to the axles, and not even four horses could pull them out. One farmer had two buffalo. They

3

hooked up the two buffalo to the wagon and tested what they could do. The two buffalo went on their knees and inched the wagon out of the mud.

Several pictures of buildings and people are taken from a book about my village called Heidendorfer Heimatbuch by Kurt Csallner with permission from Hermann Schuller, Chairman, Hilfskomitee der Siebenbuerger Sachsen.

(Picture from the Csallner book.[1])
The Lutheran church that I attended.

There was just one phone in our village, and it was located in the mayor's office. It was used to communicate from village to village and to receive reports of inclement weather. The church bell was used to let the people know that catastrophic weather was coming. We had a town crier who announced news

---

[1]   Kurt Csallner, Heidendorfer Heimatbuch, Hilfskomitee der Siebenbuerger Sachen (Schweinfurt: Schweinfurter Druckerei und Verlagsanstalt, 1969), 95.

by beating a drum and calling out, "Hear ye, hear ye." But by the time he let everybody know that bad weather was coming, it was too late.

The bells were also used to call people to church. At 10:00 A.M. one bell would ring. Then fifteen minutes later another bell would sound; then after another fifteen minutes all three bells would ring. I remember that we, as young children, would walk in front of our parents when it was time for everyone to go to church. I helped pull the ropes to ring the bells, and they sounded so heavenly.

I also helped in pumping air for our church organ. Sometimes I was distracted. There would be no air and the organist would call out, "What's the matter?" Everyone would look up. I was so embarrassed.

In our village there were only about 160 houses. The houses were numbered and we had only four street names. Our house was number 153 on Mill Street. If you were to talk about someone, you would have to refer to their house number, because we had so many Schusters, Schmitts, and Schneiders.

The house I was born in; I am on the horse.

In our house there was as an earthen floor, and we all slept on straw mattresses on our beds in the living room. The mattresses were prickly at first but in time, the straw got softer. When I was on my straw bed, I thought that underneath my bed there was a "boogieman." For years, I never let my feet dangle off my bed. I never ended up finding a boogieman under my bed. My parents never told me about him; I just had a feeling of it. I must have heard it from someone.

To bathe ourselves, we used a barrel cut in half and filled three quarters full of good, warm water. The smallest one got in first; the last one was my dad. Mom made her own soap, and we used the same soap for washing our clothes and ourselves. Mom washed our clothes in the river. We did not have clocks or calendars.

I went to school where I studied two languages, German and Romanian, as well as history, geography, mathematics, and religion. Each subject was one hour long. At school, meetings, and church High German was spoken. I learned the Saxon German dialect from my parents. It was spoken in my home and with villagers. The fourth language I spoke, Hungarian, was taught to me by a miller who worked for my father. If necessary, we all could speak that language. We did.

(Picture from the Csallner book.[2])
My schoolhouse.

---

2   Kurt Csallner, Heidendorfer Heimatbuch, Hilfskomitee der Siebenbuerger Sachen (Schweinfurt: Schweinfurter Druckerei und Verlagsanstalt, 1969), 16.

The school teacher, who taught all subjects including religion, was a very strict disciplinarian. She punished the boys by whipping them on the behind with a cane. The girls got the whipping on the hand. Severe whippings were on the fingertips with the fingers closed together. My teacher would also watch us on the grounds and on the street beside a parent. If she saw students misbehave, she would have a talk with them. So students had better behave themselves. While I was in school, I never heard of a student being sent to a principal for discipline. My teacher was there for that.

My school year picture; I am standing directly underneath my teacher.

We didn't have a library or a suspension. There was also no tardiness. I never heard of vacation or looking forward to when we would be free from school. The first time I heard and understood what it was, I was in Canada. We didn't have a dress code, but no sloppy clothes or pants were allowed. Children went to school with clean clothes and dressed properly and had an attitude of being behaved.

When we were growing up, there was much to be learned outside of school. Girls and boys met in groups for both getting work done and learning skills. We got to know each other this way. As we grew older the boys learned about farming, some woodworking, how and when to do things, and how to tie bags of grain. The girls had to learn about housekeeping, cooking, baking, and looking after babies. They learned sewing and also how to use the loom. They had to learn how to bake bread and how the dough had to be kneaded until ready. The oven was preheated and the dough went in on a long stick with a flat round piece for the dough to lie on. Mom knew when the bread was ready.

My oldest sister Maria belonged to a singing group. In our village, they went visiting members of the singing group. Before the girls were to sing, there was work to be done. Everybody grew corn to feed their animals, so the farmers had to bring the corn in the house and put it in the middle of the room. Everybody would sit around it and shell the husks off the cobs. Then the farmers would take the corn outside to dry in an airy bin. When good and dry they would borrow a sheller when needed to shell the corn to bring the corn to the mill. When they started to sing, I would whistle, which I enjoyed very much. At one point, I stopped whistling, and they stopped singing and asked, "Why did you stop?" I said, "I don't know the second verse." They laughed and said, "John, the melodies are the same."

My oldest sister, Maria, getting married to John Zautner.

As time went by my older sister Maria married John Zautner, a man from out of town. He was a locomotive engineer. The village band gave a customary farewell march to the young married couple as they left the village. For a wedding gift, my father gave them a heifer. They had to tie their heifer to their wagon. One day when my sister was milking the cows, one of them got loose, charged her and pinned her up against the wall. Luckily the horns were to the front, and she was not hurt.

My second oldest sister, Sophie, married John Bidner, a cabinetmaker who lived in (house) #2 in my village. He had a good mom; she had two daughters, Sophie and Katherine. Sophie married a man by the name of Martin Rauh, and they had a son by the same name. Years later they had a tobacco farm after immigrating to Ontario, Canada. Katherine was married to Michael Wolf, and they had a son by the same name. Michael Wolf's father was drafted into the German army and was killed at the Russian front. Years later, Katherine got remarried to a man she knew for many years. They both were alone so they decided to marry. His name was Martin Kirr, and he passed on some years ago. Today, Katherine lives in a home for the elderly in Tilsonburg, Ontario.

While growing up I never saw anyone marry an outsider. I remember, one time while I was in the Carpathian Mountains, there were German villages where there were not enough men or women to go around. Therefore, they inter-married with the Romanians.

The millstone. Standing to the right, a good gypsy friend; in the middle, my brother Michael. I am on the left.

I helped my father at the mill which he managed. One set of double stones was used to grind wheat into flour which was then raised on a cup elevator to the sifter. Two more sets of double stones were used to grind corn and other grains for feed. I remember one year when we got two new millstones. My brother Michael sharpened the one, and I the other. We swept the chips off. When we finished preparing the stones, we rolled them to the main ladder beam where a rope was tied to the stone. Men from the village helped us. Dad would count while one group of men would pull and another group of men would push the stone. Inch by inch the stones were rolled into place. Dad was operating the crane and lowered the stone to rest on the bottom, lining up to the five-inch hole in the middle of each stone, which would receive a four-inch shaft. The manufacturer made the side holes for the crane. Both the upper and lower stones needed balancing. The crane placed the upper stone on a gadget that used a four-inch shaft to turn the stone. The stone rotated, working against the bottom stone which did not turn, to grind the grain into three consistencies: course, fine, and very fine. The bottom stone was bolted 5 inches from the floor. The frame was put on both stones. Then we ran a couple of bags of grain through just to clean the chips from the stones.

One night Dad was working in the mill, and he stepped out for a smoke. He noticed that it was unusually cold for that time of the year. He stopped the mill and came back in the house and woke everyone up to go outside. We all had to take manure with straw and place it under each tree. Then my dad would light the straw in the manure. The smoke prevented the frost from ruining the trees in bloom. We didn't have matches. We would find two special stones, and with a wick between them, chip away until the wick lit. Then we would blow on the straw near the wick, and the glow would get bigger. This way we could have a fire or light a cigarette.

The mill is on the right.
This lady is the godmother of the gypsy baby.

If we were needed at home or in the mill, the lights would be flashed on and off. For my third oldest sister, Rosie, it would flash once. For me it would flash twice.

Next to the house was a dug out room with a few storage shelves for food. Otherwise, the food would be stored on the floor. The dug out room was cold and a great place to store food. In the middle of the yard was a manure pile.

Some of the Romanian, Hungarian and German farmers were better off than others. As customers of our mill, people brought us smoked sausages and ham so we would have meat. We would keep the meat in the dugout. These farmers were so good to us that we did not charge them for our work. Dad never charged persons that carried bags on their backs.

An incident at the mill affected my schooling. One day I saw my dad break the ice loose from the waterwheel (five or six shovels full of water), by stepping on the flywheel and turning the wheel in the opposite direction. There were many different sizes of gears; stepping on the speed wheel would create great pressure on the waterwheel. It was very dangerous. Once it was running again my dad looked at me and said, "Don't you ever do that!" All I could say was, "OK!"

That same winter it happened to me. Dad was not at home, and we had customers waiting. I found out that the slower the waterwheel ran the sooner it would freeze up. I did exactly what my father told me not to do. I was not so lucky, though. The water pressure on the waterwheel caused it to break loose. I stood next to the flywheel ready to step on it and suddenly the flywheel started to turn and I lost my balance and fell into the flywheel. I was thrown headfirst seven or eight feet into a horizontal beam. I could have been killed. It wasn't until sixty years later that my doctor told me that my nose was broken from that fall.

A customer carried me into the house. Mom put me to bed and cared for me. She put about ten hot bricks around me just to keep me warm. When Dad came home and saw that the mill was not running, I told him what had happened. He said, "It serves you right. If you don't want to listen, you have to feel it." Because of this incident, I began to stutter, and it affected my schoolwork. I had a rough time getting words out to express myself. I was a shy boy and was always afraid of saying the wrong words. I failed two grades but was able to go as far as grade six. My favorite subjects were history, geography, and mathematics. I left school in the sixth grade to work in the mill. That ended my formal education. The more work I was able to do the less help my father had to hire. With the pressure of school gone, my stuttering subsided and eventually was gone. I felt awful that I failed two grades.

In the wintertime we threw snowballs at each other. I've seen many times where people would hook up their horses to the other person's sleigh and have some fun in the snow.

In our village we had a Jewish family who ran a dry goods store. The parents had one daughter and one son. On Friday at sundown until Saturday at sunset they wouldn't handle any money. To buy something, customers would lay the money on the counter. The son would tell them what change to take. They were very well-respected people.

We had gypsies living on our Mill Street. One was a blacksmith. The family included a son my age who was a good friend. Both the wagon maker and the blacksmith worked together (they were brothers-in-law). We had a barber who went everyday to cut hair in the village. There was a shoemaker who repaired shoes for other people as well as his family. There was a musician. They were all fine people. Their children went to our school and our Lutheran Church.

We also had some traveling gypsies who lived in their covered wagons. They always asked my dad if he would allow them to park on the riverbank. They used the river water to drink. If they could set up shop, they would make a copper ring for my sister Rose and others. I'm not sure if Rose still has one. When it was time for them to leave, my dad would ask why they were not leaving, and they said they liked it there. My dad would give them 24 more hours. When there was no sign of then leaving, my dad went to our mayor who then summoned all the farmers to the mill. They came with their shovels, pitchforks, etc., but no harm was ever done. They packed up and left.

In our village in the springtime, we had a custom; four herdsmen boys would gather the animals to guide them to the good pastures in the hills. The boys would start at one end of the village; one would get the calves, another would get the pigs, and the other two, the lambs and sheep. This was done every other day for a week. The herdsmen would come down from the hills to get food from the people who had any animals there and water from the river. Some shepherds had areas with wellsprings. They would come to the village to pick up food such as cheeses and smoked sausages, as that would only last a few days. In the fall, they would bring the animals down out of the hills much fatter than when they left. The cattle were in the hills for about four months.

My life growing up consisted mostly of working in the mill. When farmers brought their grain to the mill, I made feed for their animals. From wheat I made flour for baking bread and pastries. I had very little social life.

I thank God for my parents. They did the best they knew how. We had no money, but most often we had food, a house, a bed to sleep in, and a place to call home. We loved our parents and they loved us. At home I never heard my dad tell my mom that he loved her; I guess he proved it, as they had five children. I know no one spoke about sex or love. In school the teacher told us there was a way to reproduce. When we were small we would ask our parents where children came from. They knew the answer: "The stork brings them just in time." While growing up I never heard of rape or divorce.

When I would get something in my eye and we couldn't get it out, my mother would send me to a woman that was nursing her baby. The woman told me that she could help; she told me, "Sit in a chair and close your eyes." She then leaned over me, squirted her breast milk into my eye, moved my eye all around, dried it off and then said it was all right. And it was! It was clear and it felt good.

We had many straw-decked houses in the village. On Saturday afternoons it was our custom to sweep the front of our house. Also, we cleaned and repaired the mill from top to bottom and shined our shoes for Sunday. Remember what God said, "Be still. Know that I am God." Sunday was a day of rest.

(From the Csallner book.[3])
These young people are dressed in our Transylvanian Saxon costume worn for dances and church. My sister Rose is in the second row from the front on the far right with a black dot on her apron.

The two young ladies dressed in the Saxon dress are from my village. The other two are from the city of Bistritz. Second from the left is one of my nieces. Saxon dresses were made by mothers with help from daughters.

---

3   Kurt Csallner, Heidendorfer Heimatbuch, Hilfskomitee der Siebenbuerger Sachen (Schweinfurt: Schweinfurter Druckerei und Verlagsanstalt, 1969), 128.

Maja Nielsen kindly gave permission to reproduce two photos copyrighted by her grandfather, Oskar Netoliczka of Penzberg, Germany and printed in a book by Heinrich Zillich called Siebenbürgen. Ein abendländisches Schicksal.

(From the Zillich book.[4])
The ladies wore, for church only, the tubs on the top of their heads. The men
wore this dress for summer, and for winter the men wore sheepskin coats.

When about fifteen years old, I went to confirmation classes for a year and was confirmed into the Lutheran faith. There was no other teaching to elaborate the word of God. It was then that I could go out and socialize. Once confirmed, one could belong to the Bruderschaft which simply meant brotherhood for young men. For girls, it was sisterhood. After the confirmation a girl was allowed to wear, to church only, a tub on her head with five or six strips hanging down her back. When a girl became engaged, her mom would sew a white crown on her tub. The Sunday after being married, she wore a flat piece on her head. In the winter, a man wore a sheepskin coat for marriage, and in summer, a long white shirt with long sleeves and a wide black belt. These young people were the "cream of the crop."

---

4   Photo copyrighted by Oskar Netoliczka, Penzberg, Germany. In: Heinrich Zillich, Siebenbürgen. Ein abendländisches Schicksal (Königstein im Taunus: Langewiesche, 1957), 3.

(From the Csallner book.[5])

Emmerichs	Breckners
The day of Emmerich's marriage.	The day after the Breckner's marriage.

I know both couples, the Emmerichs and the Breckners.

There was a dance hall in our village where the mothers would go and look over the boys and girls to see which would match their son or daughter. My parents had a different girl in mind for me. Her parents were our customers at the mill but they lived in another village. Most of the time they brought her with them, but I never had a chance to go for a walk with her. We were just confirmed, and I did not have a chance to dance with her. (Anyway, I was too shy to ask). As circumstances were, we all became refugees, and I never heard from her or saw her again.

One day I was having a drink in a hotel, and my dad walked in and sat at the bar. All he had to do was to look at me and motion to get out; even though I just ordered a spritzer (similar to 7-Up). I guess my dad couldn't see us together in the same hotel. He was my father and I had no problem with that.

I remember Dad seeming frustrated much of the time. Looking back now, I can understand why. He couldn't get ahead; it was always the same

---

5   Kurt Csallner, Heidendorfer Heimatbuch, Hilfskomitee der Siebenbuerger Sachen (Schweinfurt: Schweinfurter Druckerei und Verlagsanstalt, 1969), 11.

routine for him. If I hadn't immigrated to Canada I would have fallen into the same rut—having nothing. I remember asking Dad for a quarter to go to the circus. He hesitated, because money was always in such short supply, but he gave it to me anyway, and said, "Whatever is left over, bring home." As a result I didn't go.

My dad was a good dad. His heart was in the right place, even though occasionally he struggled with drinking. My dad was sorry about the things that happened when he would drink. I never saw him lash out at my mom or at his family. My father worked in the mill and my mother took care of the family. As the children grew older everyone helped in the mill.

Mom, like all the women in the village, made clothes for our family. She had a 'web stool' (loom) for making material for clothing.

Using a spinning wheel like this, I was taught how to spin.

Yarn was made from the flax plant, which grew to four or five feet. When it ripened, it was cut as close to the ground as possible. Then the plants were tied into bundles and laid in the riverbed with heavy boulders on them for four or five weeks. I have seen some of them—not ours—float down the river if they were not secured with enough boulders. When good and soft, the bundles were brought out to dry. When dry, the plants were broken from end to end and the fibers combed out. The yarn was then spun from those fibers. I learned to spin those fibers into thread.

In that same river we did a lot of things. We went swimming, but we did not have bathing suits—just an apron tied around us. The ladies had an extra apron to put on. The water was deeper around the waterwheel, six to seven feet deep, and my family saved many people from drowning.

I always liked catching fish. I swam over to the roots of a big tree where the bigger fish were caught. I fished until one day a crab bit my finger. That was the end of my fishing. We also bathed our horses in that river. We rode them into the deep water. When I saw the horse I was riding having a hard time swimming, I would jump off and swim to lighten the load. We had lots of fun in the water. We had a screen across the water in front of the waterwheel to catch old branches and leaves to prevent them from getting tangled in the water wheel. Every now and then we had to pull off a section of the screen to clean it.

One day my sister Rose and her lady friend swam above the mill in the deep water. The strong current took her into the water wheel. Fortunately, she was swept onto the waterwheel shovels and not in the other direction where she would have been crushed. From that day on, the screen was left in place all the time. No one knew how to move it except my dad, our helper, and me.

Mom baked pastries and bread. She milked cows and made butter and cottage cheese. Two of my older sisters were married before I was a teenager. We were a poor family. No one got paid for his or her labor. Everyone worked for the common cause. My father bartered for his milling work with grain, and then he would sell this for cash. I remember a saying posted on the wall of the mill: If you are satisfied with my performance, tell others; if you are not satisfied, tell me.

Dad liked to entertain customers with stories from when he was in World War I and had become an officer in the Hungarian army. In our village it was very seldom that you would see a car or airplane. One day while he was telling these stories, it happened that a military plane flew over us. One of our customers asked my father if he would like to take a chance and ride in an airplane, and Dad said, "Oh, yeah. Oh, yeah. Sure, as long as I can keep one foot on the ground!"

Basically, money changes everything: appearance, clothing and lifestyle. People were kinder and more respectful when I was young. Things were different. People were poorer; we were in a war. I have always tried to open the door for a lady and would often give up my seat for a lady as well.

(From the Zillich book.[6])
A large Lutheran church; I have been there many times.

I used to walk on the railroad track many times, barefooted. Sometimes I would slide off the track and dash my toes on a sharp stone. I would have a gash. I would wonder what I was going to do, go back home or go on to my aunt's house. Along the railroad track, every so often, there was a hut on the side for protection from the weather. There, also, bundles of branches were laid along the railroad tracks just in case of a runaway car. A man working for the railroad would run and throw some of those branches across the railroad track. Every time the railroad car would go over some of the bundles of the branches, the railroad car would slow down. The man was available all the time; he lived near the tracks. The train came and went two to four times a day. The closer to the city, the more huts and branches there were for stopping the train. These trains didn't have air brakes, as we have them now.

---

6   Photo copyrighted by Oskar Netoliczka, Penzberg, Germany. In: Heinrich Zillich, Siebenbürgen. Ein abendländisches Schicksal (Königstein im Taunus: Langewiesche, 1957), 6.

A city by the name of Bistritz was only 5 kilometers (3 miles) to the east from my village. At one time part of the city burned down. Sickness went through the whole area and many people died.

Doctors and hospitals were located there. My aunts, uncles, nieces and nephews lived there. Also, there was a large Lutheran church. My dad's brother was the watchman for the whole city. There was a walkway around the church from where one could see the surroundings for miles. He watched for fires. For a fire there was a loud bell sound, and the fire department looked up to get directions from my uncle. He would point them to the direction they should go. As children, we would play hide and seek up there. My uncle had just a bedroom with changes of clothing. In winter he had a coal stove. There was a spiral staircase of about three hundred steps leading up to his room. His children would bring him food and water. While he was eating, they would be on the lookout. No one had a phone in Bistritz, except for one in the city hall. This office received reports of inclement weather.

People helped each other. When a person had a toothache, he would be tied to a tree and given all the whiskey he could drink. The person would pass out, and then the man who saw how they pulled teeth in the Russian army would get a pair of pliers and pull the tooth. When the person became sober and the pain was still great, more whiskey was given to dull the pain.

I wanted to learn as much about milling as possible. This included clearing the ice formation from the riverbed to have a clear water flow away from the waterwheel. We had to start at the far end, work ourselves up close to the waterwheel. We all had to chip away at the ice to make smaller pieces. We had a long rod with an iron tip; this would split the ice well, depending on the thickness of it. One day my mom called us for dinner. I was on a huge chunk of ice, and when I looked up at Mom, I slipped into the icy water. Once I went under the ice I didn't feel a thing. Our man Gabor jumped in after me and got hold of my leg. He tried to break the ice loose with his head. The ice finally broke loose, and he brought me out of the water. Mom brought two blankets for us; one for the hired help and one for me. Gabor put me to bed. He worked for us for years. Then Mom put ten hot bricks around me to keep me warm. The next morning I went to work. I didn't have any other jobs while growing up.

In 1932–1933 there was a cloudburst that caused the levee to break and resulted in the biggest flood I had ever seen. This dam diverted the water from one direction to another. The dam broke because of too much excess water. It couldn't hold it. I remember there was a single man living with his chickens and two pigs. His house was surrounded by high water, so he tied a rope around the belly of one pig, went up on the roof of his house, then pulled his pig up and sat on top of his house with his pig. The fire department where my father volunteered was called to rescue him. The firefighter threw a rope to him and told him to tie it around his waist and go to the end of the house. The firefighter had one end of the rope tied to a tree. The man debated about his pig because that was all he had, but the firefighter had no choice but to pull him into the rushing water. The man was taken to a higher level and the people looked after him. His two pigs and chickens drowned.

Our house was somewhat higher. We had maybe 130 people in the house; some were standing on the porch, and some were outside in the rain. I am not sure if any people were lost. I remember that many bridges and railroad tracks were washed out. There was a total shutdown. During the flood we didn't have school or church. We had no electricity as everything was at a standstill. After the rain, when the water subsided, the farmers hauled heavy rocks, boulders and long heavy branches from our forest to repair our levee. It took weeks but finally it was done and we could run the mill and have electricity.

In 1933-1934 we had the depression. There was no work, no money. Farmers were lucky to have their livestock to kill; this helped them survive. My mom made bread out of oat flour. I'm not sure if any people died. In the winter we had to be very careful to keep the waterwheel rolling, otherwise it would freeze up. Many times we would get customers from other mills because their waterwheel had frozen up. If so, with the shovels full of water there was great pressure on the waterwheel. By adding hot water on both sides of the waterwheel walls (my dad would ask our neighbors to bring their hot water to the mill), all of a sudden the ice would break loose. We had the mill running 24 hours a day. We let the waterwheel turn very slowly, just slow enough to slide the belt onto the wheel. The flywheel drove the generator, so everybody would have electricity and the flywheel kept the speed. Every night we pulled the switch for the village and it was in darkness, except we had electricity in the mill. We had the lights on at dusk until 10:00 P.M. in the winter and until 11:00 P.M. in the summer.

When there was a funeral or a wedding and the electricity was needed for two to three hours longer, a permit would have to be acquired from the mayor to supply electricity for that period of time. At weddings and funerals we usually received a plate full of food and a bottle of wine for our services from those involved.

My dad was the oilier for the gears of the mill. One day when he was oiling, he reached over the transmission and his shirt got caught in the transmission. His shirt wound up until he had to brace himself on a beam above and tear it off his back. At another mill a shorter man was not so lucky. He was found swinging around the transmission; he was dead.

In 1918 Romanians and Hungarians made an agreement that the Romanians could have Transylvania until 1940. One day I saw a Hungarian officer riding on a beautiful horse through our village. Everybody asked, "Why are the Hungarians marching in our village?" We learned all this in our history class in school. I have never forgotten that. In a few days, the schools had new Hungarian schoolbooks. The teacher was bilingual. One day at a dance a man got drunk and said that he will not speak the Hungarian language. The Hungarian told him, "As long as you breathe Hungarian air, you will speak Hungarian!"

One day a Hungarian official came to my dad. He made my dad an offer that he could have all the land he could supervise (help included) if my dad would become a Hungarian and denounce being German. My dad told this Hungarian official flat out, "NO! We will remain German." He never even asked his family. I understand that the Hungarian could not see that a man with a real Hungarian name would be German. They tried to do everything to win us over. I am glad that my dad stood his ground. Looking back, if he had become Hungarian, we probably would not have had to flee the country.

I wonder if anyone could imagine if my dad had had a change of heart and become Hungarian. I'm sure I would have been drafted into the Hungarian army (I knew the language). I would have missed all the fine people in my life, and would not have lived in Austria or Germany or immigrated to Canada; I would not have had a chance to have two farms, but before all of that, my family that I loved, especially my dear wife, my two boys and my dear daughter. I would not have met the Srigleys or Fausts, and oh yes, the Gedkes; the business people I had and so many other people like John Johnson and family, the Asches and the Shoemakers. May the good Lord be with you all.

We had many Romanian, Hungarian, and German farmers as customers at our mill. Every year one or the other would invite us to come visit them. We would borrow a wagon with a horse and put lots of straw in it. Dad would drive with Mom next to him. My sister Rose, my brother

Michael, and I would get into the back of the wagon. If it was later in the year we would prepare ourselves with hot bricks wrapped in bags and put them in the wagon to keep us children warm. Our parents each had two hot bricks underneath their feet. After an hour and a half ride, we arrived and they were waiting for us. On this trip, we stopped at a nice big farm. This farmer was also one of our good customers. His name was Berlan Pompei. I remember him so well. The family set a large table with good meals and drinks for all. Wine was made in our village. We all spoke the Romanian language. Other farmers from the same village came over. As they were glad, we stopped by to visit them.

The day went fast, and before we left they gave us smoked sausages, ham and lots of cheese, kept our bricks hot, and fed the horse. We were loaded with food to take home. On our way home, we, the children, laid on the warm bricks covered with straw, a nice bed to sleep on. Mom and Dad leaned on each other and slept—the horse knew the way home. We covered ourselves with blankets. It never failed to rain, and by the time we got home, we were soaking wet. When we woke up the only way we knew how long we had been at home was by the mound the horse left behind. The horse was not ours. One would think the horse was ours as it came to our house when it should have gone to its own home. That is what I call horse sense. Nevertheless, we had a good time, which made it all worthwhile. Visiting the people got us more customers, and that is customer relations. Every year we went to a different village.

Our farmers sold their products to the resorts in the Carpathian Mountains, which were four hours to the east, by a horse-drawn wagon. The wines produced in our village were also sold to the resorts and to other villages and cities. One couple took me with them to the Carpathian Mountains to care for their horses.

I remember Thanksgiving Day at home in Transylvania. There were no turkeys. We would get roosters fattened up for weeks and put them in a little fenced-in pen. At Thanksgiving, people would gather together, and one man would be blind-folded, given a club, and put in the pen with a rooster. At the sound of the rooster, he would swing the club, and the man who killed the rooster could keep it for Thanksgiving dinner.

At Easter everyone received an orange. My sister Rose received all of our peels. She would put them in a jar of water, and after a few weeks the water would turn orange. In time my sister would use it as a perfume. Oh, by the way, my sister was a kindergarten teacher.

I remember Christmas, also. Nothing compared to the Christmas tree we had at home. It was a small tree with snap-on candles which we would light. We had apples and baked items on the tree. We couldn't wait for Santa Claus to come (Santa was our neighbor). He came in with bells tied around his belly and with a couple of thin branches and a bag full of surprises. He asked us children if we had been good. Yes, we were good, we said. Though sometimes I got spanked with those branches and was told not to say or do something anymore, Santa would give each of us two or three nuts. Before he left, Dad would give him a shot of whiskey. For dinner we would eat whatever we had.

I knew of a few boys in our village with hardly anything to eat. If a boy wanted to surprise his mother, he would eat an apple to the core, tie a string to the core and throw it to the geese. Once the goose swallowed it the boy would pull the goose in and put it under his coat to sneak it home.

Husbands drafted into the German Army saying goodbye to their wives and children.

I remember in 1941-1942 thousands of our men were drafted into the German Army. The time came for them to gather at the railroad station in the city of Bistritz. Before the men boarded the train, the Lutheran minister and Catholic priest prayed that the Lord would be with them to protect and watch over them. The men started boarding the train and singing a German Christian song that went like this. "We praise you, O God, our Redeemer, Creator, in grateful devotion our tribute we bring.

We lay it before You, we kneel and adore You. We bless Your holy name, glad praises we sing." If all the tears could have been gathered, it would be called a river of tears.

The women with children came home fearing that all the farm work and upcoming harvest had to be done, so we would all have to chip in. Here on these farms, I learned how to use a scythe. The farmers were mostly older, disabled, and old men. We all worked very hard to get all the harvest done. There was only one farmer, named Ruhrig, who had a threshing machine and a tractor. Every farmer had to bring all their sheaves to the threshing machine. Everyone had a spot to unload; the able men would load up their grain into the farmer's wagons in bags. So it was with the straw. In the evening the women had to milk the cows. Every day the days seemed to have gotten longer and longer. We left many wheat ears on the fields so the poor people would go and glean them; thresh the wheat out with a flail, and then they had wheat for months. The more they gathered, the more they had. They had to bring it to the mill to make flour. They all had to carry their bags. Dad never charged them.

Once the harvest was done a couple of my friends went to the Carpathian Mountains to explore. We went to the other side of the mountains. We were in Bukovina, Russia, and there were no big mountains. The German army was close to Moscow when their orders came to withdraw to go fight the United States in North Africa. In 1941-42 on the way west, they ran out of food and had no warm clothes. They all froze to death. Someone would urinate which would then freeze up before it even hit the ground.

Our band always needed new players so I volunteered. I had to learn the notes. We practiced often so that after two or three more times of practice, I would have been ready to play in the band. I played the trombone for funerals because it was a slow march. The Lutheran minister would walk behind the band and the hearse drawn by two black horses. At the grave site men carried the coffin, followed by the bereaved family and friends. Our band played at the grave site. If it was a man's funeral the band would play *ich hat einen Kameraden*, in English *I Had a Comrade*. This band also played for dances and weddings. In the beginning of the 1940's, we had Germans marching through our villages and our men started to trade with the Germans. They would supply our family farms with plows in exchange for our products like apples, pears, plums and prunes.

In 1943, the custom was that a boy asked the girl that he had a crush on, if she would allow him to plant a May tree in front of her bedroom window. I was surprised that a girl would allow me. That winter towards spring two to three boys went in the forest to select May trees and marked them. In May we helped each other plant a May tree in the middle of the night. When we were finished, her father, the mayor of our village, came out and invited all of us in for a drink.

The following Sunday, Sophie came to me and asked if I would sit next to her in the church. She pinned a nice corsage on my lapel. I didn't remember a word the minister said. I was eager to hear the last word, "Amen." That afternoon we went dancing. Through occasions like this many marriages occurred. Our romance time was cut short after a while. We all became refugees, and we lost track of each other.

Dad knew seven languages. I wish I had asked him more questions and drew from his wide area of knowledge. Dad did teach me many things, though. When we bought new belts for our mill, Dad taught me how to shave off one side of both ends of the belts, clamp them together in a vice and fasten them together with leather straps. By seventeen years of age, I knew how to operate the mill by myself. Dad knew his business and was a well-known miller in the area; he was known as one who did quality work. Dad wanted to instill all his knowledge in me, and I was very proud of him.

One morning my dad went in the mill and found that our new belts were stolen. His Dad reported it right away to the mayor and the gendarme (police). The only way to find the thief was by leaving ten to twelve young girls and boys to watch all night if necessary, and I was one of them. We had a 2 1/2 ft. deep barrel of water and waited until the water was nice and calm. We all knelt around and a white sheet was put over our heads. One girl saw a man coming through the waterwheel door. Another girl saw him go to the new belts. He cut the one, rolled it up and put it in a large bag. Another girl after a while saw that the man (robber) had a hard time getting up the hill. Another one said that the man stood in front of the village's water well. This water is only for human consumption. My dad stopped everything. He knew who stole those belts. The following morning my father, the police, and I found the belts. Before the police arrested him, the thief had to take all the belts he had stolen, from one end of our village to the other end. Many people knew him because he worked for my family. Another man who worked on the farm stole smoked sausage meat. He too was caught. He had to carry all the stolen goods on his neck from one end of the village to the other. They never found another job in our village. What an embarrassment!

About the practice of looking into two and one half feet of water to find a robber for stealing, I never heard of it before I was seventeen years old. Why would they want young people to look into the barrel? We were too young to imagine things like that. We had other things to worry about as we were in a war, all I could see was the hill the robber had to climb. I surmise our people used this kind of practice, otherwise how would they know as we had no police dogs to search for the robber. When we got our belts back it took a few days to put them together.

In the meantime, a slew of covered wagons drove in one after the other. Their leader asked my dad if he spoke German. They all had white wheat to make flour, which took a few hours. My dad did not charge them anything. My dad asked where they came from; they said they were Germans from the Volga River region in Russia. Dad wished them all well as one after another left. My dad turned to me and said that he hopes that this will not happen to us, but it surely did. (About 60 years later, I attended a Mennonite Brethren Church in Ontario. Most of the people came also from the Volga River. I did not find any one that came through my part of the world.)

On September 17th, 1944 the town crier went to every second or third house to call out with his drum, "Hear ye, hear ye. Orders just came in to get ourselves ready. We have to flee our homes." People cried and clung to each other asking what is going to happen to us? People put covers on the wagons, greased them, and shod the horses. People killed their animals and fried them. They put them in five-gallon crocks, poured hot lard over to seal them. We had to flee the Russians; if we did not, we would end up in Siberia in the coal mines. I met German women who were there. I met them in Canada; they were married and had families. Wherever the military goes, they have everybody under their control. I met some Russian girls; they were brought by German officers.

One of our men was drafted in the Romanian army. Then, a miller and my dad were drafted into the Hungarian army. I have never been so scared in my life.

I had my physical to go into the German army. I was accepted. The mayor of my village came to me. He asked how well I knew how to operate the mill. I told him, "100%." "Good," he said. He instructed me to give him the draft papers once I received them. He told me that because we had a good harvest, he did not want to leave it to the Russians. Therefore, he wanted me to stay home to make flour for the German army. Eight other men would bring all the wheat to me to make flour. They had to feed millions of people, military and civilians. They also picked up our animals for meat. I had a good gypsy friend who knew how to run the mill by day. If trouble arose, he would have to wake me.

I knew that I had to work alone. I then covered all windows with burlap bags and locked the front door. I had only one light burning because I knew my way around, in the half darkness. No one dared to go past the water wheel because it was slippery and dangerous. It was also the shortest way to start and to stop the mill, especially on rainy days or bitter cold.

Then on September 20, 1944, the whole village had to follow one wagon after another. On my mom's wagon there were my two sisters, Sophie and her son John Bidner, my other sister Rose and my two-year younger brother Michael. Was it ever hard to say goodbye. We didn't know if we were going to see each other again. They all gathered on our large soccer field, and the Lutheran minister prayed for a safe journey. The leader was one of our men who was in the German army. He was wounded on the Russian front, but was good enough to ride his German motorcycle. He told us that he will see to it that we stay sometimes in large rooms. His name was Martin Shuster. He received his orders from the German Army. On the way out of our village, church bells rang, they sounded so heavenly. We hoped that it would not be the last time. Mom's convoy soon found out that their wagons were not prepared with brakes. They found out when they had to go downhill; their horses were not able to hold the wagons back. Therefore, some of the men went in the forest to cut two long trees the size of a man's leg. They had a chance to put the beam at the wheel. Not much problem going downhill. It took them hours by eighty wagons. Or they would put the beams between the spokes so the two wheels would not turn. That was the best way.

My dad in the Hungarian army in WW II.

At night I was the only one working. After the second night alone, I was so tired; I filled the hopper with wheat knowing the bell would ring to wake me when the hopper got empty. The bell fell down on the millstone; bounced on the body frame; and the stones rubbed against each other causing sparks. The sparks made a fire and had it been another two feet closer I would have been engulfed in the fire. All of a sudden, I found myself in my father's arms. I believe with all of my heart that the Almighty God nudged my dad's heart to go home and that his son might be in danger. I am so glad that my dad listened to that still small voice. Before my father came up to me, he threw the belt off that turned the millstone and stopped it. Then he used the water in the five gallon pails to quench the fire, since we didn't have any plumbing. I doubt that my dad had a pass to come home because he was only in the Hungarian army for two or three weeks. He knew that if he got caught it would be the end of him, officer or not. I am not sure what my father ate since he had to hide during the day and walk at night. He was stationed about 25 km. away.

I knew where my dad was stationed. It took him several nights to come home to me. I saw Russian planes over us at night flying west. Dad came to me just in time to save me from death. I thank God for protecting my dad and me. Needless to say, I was scared but so glad to have seen my father. We dismantled everything. My dad worked on one stone and I on the other one. We had to make new curves and sharpen them because the stones were all flat. We had to start all over like brand new; it took us hours. The old wooden frame was all burned up; we took one from another double stone. We got things ready to go in the morning, and then we went to bed. I did ask my dad how he knew that I was in danger. He replied, "Something told me to go home." In the morning, my father was gone. I was so scared. The gypsy women fed us as we all knew each other.

After a few days, I got my order to get ready to leave. There were nine men and we had three wagons. We loaded ten full size bags of flour among the three wagons, which we covered with a lot of hay. In fact, my dad told me to come see him on our way to Hungary. We drove there and told the guard my name. I am the son of John Hunyady. After checking his chart, he then told me that he was transferred to another station. We drove there and were told again that my dad had been transferred to yet another station; we then went there and asked if I could see my dad. The guard told me that the military had transferred him back where he had been at first. I did not want to go back; it was too risky. I didn't want to take the chance. I might have taken the chance if I had been alone. I just didn't want to jeopardize these men's lives, as I had seen the Russian planes flying overhead. Then we had to leave. I was the only one that spoke the Hungarian language, so I was the one to contact the Red Cross. The Red Cross knew where our village convoy was. So we headed that way. Finally, close to Budapest, we caught up to our people. I felt sorry for the horses because they had gone such a long distance with hardly any rest. I was happy to be reunited with my mom, sisters, the little boy, and my brother.

I found out that fresh bread and stolen grapes tasted so good. By then, all the food that they had prepared at home was gone. Then we all had to stand in line to get our food from the German army. Many roads were not even graveled, and the horses left a deep hole behind where they stepped. I was always glad when it rained, because after the rain accumulated, many times I would sift the water out of these holes with my mouth. When you are thirsty the water is so good. I remember that when we joined my mom, I slept anywhere, even under the wagons. Sometimes it rained, and the water had no place to go and would gather under the wagon. Only the children and older people were in the wagons. When there was lightning I did not want to go into the forest. When the women left home, they brought with them the traditional clothes. If the men played in the brass band, they brought with them their instruments and their clothes. What a beautiful tradition in clothes we had. When we came to the Danube River, we let our horses drink a little at a time. I would walk in the river with my clothes on, simply to cool off. Afterwards, I felt somewhat clean. I got wet so often, the sun dried my clothes on my body. The German military kitchen was not always available where we were.

City folks didn't have any access to wagons and horses; therefore they were herded in a cattle car with no latrine facilities. They all had to relieve themselves in five gallon pails. When the pails were full they would toss them out the door. My sister and her family were taken from one station to the next in the rail cars. The rail tracks had to be opened for the German army first. Then at the mercy of a conductor their rail cars were hooked up and taken to another station. Meanwhile the German army told us to go west.

Before we entered the Hungarian desert, we loaded up with food for us and feed for the animals. After two or three days in the desert, we ran out of food, water, and feed for both the animals and us. Then we came to a large haystack; we made large bundles and laid them on the tarp that covered the wagon. One man said to the Lutheran minister that we were stealing. The minister said that God had provided.

Now in eastern Austria near Vienna, the farmers had their turnips and potato harvest. The farmers had to boil their potatoes before they were buried below the freezing ground. When needed, the turnips were chopped up first for the cows and young cattle. For the young cattle they were chopped up much finer. One evening, I wanted to get water from the trough to wash myself and the head of the house took me into the shower room to take a shower. Not having seen a shower before, I asked her, "What is that?" She told me to shed my clothes once I was in the shower. She left the bathroom once I was behind the curtain. Then she came back and reached in to adjust the water. After my shower, I slept between two clean white sheets. That was a treat for me; I had never slept in a bed like this one. This was the first time in seven weeks that I took off my underwear and clothes. They just stood up. She gave me her husband's clothes to wear; I then burned mine. Her husband was killed on the Russian front.

My dad was very sick with asthma; he had left the Hungarian army and went to Vienna. Dad inquired about us at the Red Cross. They gave him food and civilian clothes. Then one day, there was a knock on the door and I opened it up, and there stood my dad. We were so glad to be together again.

Because my dad was so sick, he felt he would not survive if he remained with the army. In case someone was looking for him, he had to devise a subterfuge. He changed the spelling of his name from John Hunyadi to John Hunyady. That way if someone inquired about him, he was not John Hunyadi, but rather John Hunyady. For the safety of the family, he told us to spell our last name as he did, Hunyady.

Before we left to continue on the journey, we filled our jugs with water. By that time, I did not have our horses because they were sick. A lady with three teenage daughters asked if she could join us and we said, "Yes." She told us that she had a Russian prisoner who could drive their tractor. Then she offered me two oxen to pull my wagon. Our men had to fabricate a different system to hook up the oxen to the wagon. She gave me many bags of feed for the oxen. Some Austrian farmers joined us in our travel to West Austria to flee the Russians.

After a few days on the road, we rested our horses and our men took that opportunity to make repairs to the wagons. We had a long convoy; our leader could not be all over at the same time. Russian airplanes attacked our people. They burned our wagons, shot and killed some of our people and horses. Our men loaded up the bodies on their wagons and in time, when we came to a Lutheran cemetery, our minister would bury the bodies there. Nobody knows how many were killed or who. Some of our horses were only wounded; the German soldiers had to do mercy killings. At my end of the convoy, only an older lady was shot in the buttocks. Her daughter-in-law saw the blood. The German medics took care of her.

Many Russian soldiers were taken into the German prison. On the way they called out, "Bread, bread!" I understood that. I gave one soldier a chunk of bread that I always had in my pocket. A German officer came and reprimanded me. By then, we were not to travel during the day because the road had to be left open for the German army. We hid our wagon under large trees. So the three boys, my brother, our friend Martin Schuster and I had nothing to do, so we tried to explore the area. We came to a large field. All of a sudden I saw twelve United States airplanes headed east. I saw white vapor trails that the airplanes leave behind. Then I could see that one airplane left the others and circled lower and lower. I said that they must have spotted us and we better run. All of a sudden there was a tree that I didn't see there before. I believe that God must have provided a tree for us.

So we hid behind the tree. I went first, then my brother and then Martin. Then the machine gun went off and hit the bottom of the tree to about seven or eight feet high. We were unharmed. After it was over, we looked at this tree and saw one bullet after another. I have seen trees of that size being split in half. The airplane was shot down. The pilot jumped with his parachute and was caught by the German army. The United States airplane was only about three hundred to four hundred feet away from us. There was the German artillery in the same forest. We had to move on.

In Austria, we worked on a farm where four or five people, maybe more, were sitting around a table. Everybody received one or two slices of bread and all had to throw pieces of bread into the bowl filled with hot milk, and then we started eating from the bowl. My sisters would not eat out of this bowl as one could see traces of milk from the bowl to each person. When done, all would wipe their spoons on the tablecloth and put their spoons under the table in their own place. My sisters ate with our parents taking food from them. One person after another started to come to the table. It did not matter anymore, the farmer's way was so good when you are hungry, and we were often hungry.

While living in that part of Austria I had a strong desire to work in a flour mill. I found one and told the man that I was experienced in milling with stones but not with rollers. He said, "We'll see." He went to two or three double rollers and set them off course. I could have the job, if I could find the rollers that were off course. I went to the second and third rollers, I found they were the ones which were off course; he then said that I could have the job. I knew many Jewish people, but you could not find a kinder man. After a few days I told this man that I had promised the German Army that whenever I moved and stayed a week at one place, I'd report to the German Army. This kind man said we are making flour for the military and civilians; therefore, I should stay because we work for one and one for all. I knew what this meant. After a few more days I had to move on. He was a good man and was sorry when we had to part. We embraced each other and wished each other well and I thanked him for saving my life and for not letting me go into the German Army.

While my sister Maria and family were waiting at a train station to be hooked up to be taken to another station, the Russians caught up to them. They asked them in German, "From where do you come from?" Someone told them, "Bistritz." They took the family back to Transylvania Bistritz, where my brother-in-law dug graves for that city for years. As years went by they tried to get out of Romania. Finally, the Russians let them out.

They ended up in Leverkusen near Cologne, Germany. They all worked for the Bayer Aspirin Company. The company supplied every family with a house to live in. I visited them in 1979, and in 1983 my sister Rose and I saw them again.

This is my oldest sister Maria's burial place in Germany.

In 1945 we were on the west end of Austria, and we stopped there for approximately three months. We were not sure where to go from there. My parents did not work, but my sisters, my brother, my nephew, John Bidner, and I lived there and found jobs on a nice, big farm. On this farm, the women did the men's jobs like feeding, breeding, cleaning, and milking.

I was taught how to plow with four horses. The farmer's daughter wanted a young man to be her chauffeur and drive her to Salzburg, Austria, in her buggy. While the farmer's daughter visited her aunt in Salzburg, she gave me money to go to the movies. Salzburg is a very old and beautiful city. It has huge thick walls surrounding the city and is a tourist attraction. (Some of my wife's brothers and sisters lived in that area unbeknownst to me at that time.) When the boss was done with his work for the day, he would change his clothes. He would put on lederhosen and a nice Austrian hat. He had a long curved pipe and would walk down the road to the country bar where he would have apple cider. I had this apple cider a few times, and it was so good.

May 1945 was the end of the war. I saw thousands of German soldiers with their hands on top of their heads being escorted into the United States prison with machine guns. It certainly was a sad day for us Germans to surrender.

A couple of men, also refugees, who were from my village in Romania, lived on farms; they took it upon themselves to go over to Germany to seek housing and work. They found German villages that were willing to take us in. We all had to sell our oxen, horses, and wagons. We could not take them with us.

In 1946, we went by train from Austria to Germany in a cattle car. We didn't have any latrines. When a female had to go to the toilet, all the women would stand around her. When a male would have to go the men would all stand around him. Then when the can was full it was thrown out the door of the train. The village people that we were assigned to were half Catholic and half Lutheran. Once we arrived in these villages we were to work on farms. It was very hard for our people who were farmers to take orders from other farmers to do this and do that, but we all had to adjust. Some of our people wanted to return to Romania, but the children were in school or at work. In time, our men asked their farmers to sell them a piglet. They fed it and in late fall they butchered it. For the next year, they asked if they could have a corner of a field. They bought one or two piglets and one steer, so they had enough meat for their family. Their family grew and as a result they needed more meat. Many of the German farmers' sons were killed. So the German soldiers, when released from the prison, worked on the farms. The soldiers made the farmers' daughters pregnant; therefore, they had become farmers. I've been at such weddings; the villages were close, so the men formed another band. They played for special occasions. Our girls dressed up in our native costumes, and the people in that part of Germany were not used to such a tradition. I remember that most of the men that were taken into the United States prison were released with a better report than the Russian prison. My brother-in-law John Bidner was released from the Russian prison.

I remember once we were settled in Germany, it started to get colder and our men went to the village officials asking for heating material. They said to go in to the forest and take all we wanted, but don't cut any trees. People would make big bundles and carry them home, and then come back for more—not sure if everyone had enough. Between my brother, my sister Rosie, and me, we made sure that our parents had wood, coal, and food. As people worked and made money, all could afford coal or wood for their stoves to keep them warm. That forest was never so clean.

I found a job in a flour mill. In this mill, I was allowed to give one kg. of wheat flour free to each poor person. There were many poor people. In the course of my job, I met a man who was also a refugee; he was from Yugoslavia. We became good friends. This mill had rollers to make flour. My job was to help in the mill when farmers came to exchange their grain. If the farmers brought wheat, I would give them wheat flour. I kept the grain and gave them chop for their cattle. The miller's son married a lady from my village. I had gone to school with her older sister and knew her family. It was while in Germany, I saw a soccer game for the first time.

There were many German women who had families at home, and because they were so poor, they did what they had to do, even sell their bodies to get cigarettes, coffee, chocolate, and food from the American soldiers. I have seen the result of that in 1979; they exchanged their goods (flour) for clothes for their family.

Rosie and I loved to dance. In time we found out that over the hill were three villages with some of our people. One day we went over the hill to a village. We heard a brass band playing familiar songs. As we walked in, all of a sudden Sophie, the girl I had asked if I could plant a May tree in front of her bedroom window, came over. We hugged and kissed. Then her spoiled brat friend came over and said that we couldn't dance. All of a sudden someone showed up and told this friend to let us dance. This was one of the beggars at the mill that told this spoiled brat to let us dance. We enjoyed each other for a short time; not having seen each other for two years. After my immigration we lost track of each other again.

Later on in 1948, I came to a mill which had a huge diesel engine; we had three diesel engineers to install it. It took days to set it up. Meanwhile, we used water turbines to run the mill, and I had never worked with turbines before. It was a fully automated mill. The mill ran 24 hours. I slept in a large room. A cleaning lady came in every day. She picked up our laundry, washed the items and cleaned our room. The truck driver shared the same room where we were sleeping. In this mill everyone had a different shift. The millers had one week to go with the driver to help distribute to the bakeries in many parts of Germany. Many millers crumbled under the weight of flour 100 kg. (220 lbs.). The driver always liked it when it was my turn because I knew how to carry a bag. My dad showed me. I had no problem going up stairs. He even asked our boss to let me work with him all the time. But the boss said, "No, the millers had to take their turn."

Gretel and I in Germany.

A miller's job is to know the flow from one roller to the other roller. Before the flour went into another roller it had to go through a sifter. The fine flour went to one side, and the bran went to another double roller. Every time the flour went into the other roller it was made finer. This mill had six to seven double rollers and was three stories high. I went up and down by a lift. One would stand on a platform, and when you wanted to go down, you would pull on a rope very slightly. When you wanted to go up, you would pull on the rope all the way. When you wanted to stop, you would just let go of the rope. My boss gave me two weeks to get acquainted with the mill and to operate it completely by myself. There were two mills in the town. My brother worked in the first mill and I worked in the second one. After church we would come together. When we met we both loved to whistle. We would whistle only marches. When the people heard us whistling, they said the Hunyady boys were coming.

While working in Germany, I had some free time, so I would go dancing. Here is where I met Gretel. She rode on my bike and I walked over to the next village so we could dance. I told her that I had received literature from different countries to immigrate, to the United States,

Canada, Australia, or Brazil. Then I told her that my sister and I had applied to immigrate to Canada.

My parents didn't live too far from where I was working. They had a bedroom and also a kitchen. I would go and see them as often as I could. I ran the mill even on Sundays. My boss said, "Whatever water is not being made use of is wasted." I knew a few of the Catholics and they had a nice choir. They were in need of tenors so I joined them. After we had practiced for a while, the music director told us that a Cardinal was coming to the area. The director made sure we all knew how to make our crosses. I had never made a cross and thought, "What have I gotten myself into?" I could not leave, as we were sitting on a raised platform. I liked their songs and the day came when we all dressed up in our Bavarian traditional dress. I had no choice but to make a cross. When I told this to my Catholic lady friend, she said that I would make a good Catholic. Gretel was also there and heard us sing. Teasing me, she said, "You made the cross just right."

My sister Rose and I chose Canada because our sister Sophie, her husband, and son had immigrated to Canada in 1948. As soon as my brother-in-law was released from the Russian prison, they made plans to immigrate to Ontario, Canada. A statement that drew me to Canada said, "Prove yourself; we are on your side." We sent them an application to immigrate. Canada accepted the application, providing that our physicals were okay. After two weeks we were accepted to go to Canada. Now we were waiting for the okay for passage to Canada. In the meantime, I traveled some more in Germany. All the cities I went through were bombed out.

When our turn came to say goodbye to our parents and our brother, it was very hard. My dad said (and I have pondered for years what it meant), "A boy takes it away and a girl brings it home." My brother said that he could not leave our parents alone to fend for themselves. My father said that he could not give us any money for our journey "but you know how to read, write, and do arithmetic." He then lifted his hands to our heads and said, "Go and use them. Remember the way you make your bed is the way you are going to lay in it." I was very nervous.

The Lutheran Church brought many immigrants over to Canada to work on Lutheran farms. We met at the Bremen harbor to board a huge ship that held about 2,000 people. After a few days on the ocean, the captain told us that in a couple of days he would show us exactly where the Titanic sank. We just could not wait. The food on board was good. Many of the passengers were seasick and fed the fish the food they ate. I did not get seasick. On the ship we slept all over with everybody like animals. No one knew anybody. At the same time I was grateful; I slept next to my sister. After eleven days on the ocean we arrived in Halifax, Nova Scotia. It was the 15th of June, 1950, and we were to go on a train.

I was happy to come to Canada and to a new adventure. My sister and I met a young girl, maybe twenty years old, and asked her where she was going. She said, "I am going to a man that I have never met. I've only seen pictures of him. He has a large farm in Saskatchewan." The farmer was waiting for the wife-to-be to come. Their parents had arranged everything.

We arrived in Toronto, Ontario and we were divided. The ones going to the west went through one door, and the ones going north went through another door. My sister and I went on the train that went south to Simcoe. The conductor made the arrangements. We rode south, and the conductor called out our names when we came to the station where we needed to get off. My sister was the first one called, and I was the last one. The conductor also called out the farmer's name, so I would know for whom I would work. I had only a small suitcase with a pair of socks and other items.

On the way to the farm, the farmer, Mr. Otterman, started to talk in English. I could not understand a word except for 'OK.' We finally arrived at his home. He had a lovely wife, who was a schoolteacher, and two adopted children. He was a dairy farmer. We attended the Lutheran Church. When they sang a song in English that I knew, I sang it in German. My wages were taken to pay for my fare which the Lutheran Church had paid.

I had my own room. I also had a few bottles of spritzer (like 7-Up). After milking we would pour the milk in a 50 lb. can. I had to take the cans and lower them in cool water. After one milkman came to pick up those milk cans, another milkman came to deliver us bottled milk.

I could not understand why we would not drink our cow's milk. Thirteen years later I had my own dairy herd. My cows were tested; therefore, I had no problem drinking fresh milk. I was a proud milk producer with quality milk. I was in the milk-weighing program to see how much a cow produces. If low, I would breed her to a good milk-producing bull. Therefore, her offspring would be a better producer.

Mr. Otterman had hundreds of turkeys to prepare for Thanksgiving. My job was to tend to those turkeys. I saw to it that they had enough feed and water. I removed the sick and dead ones. Whenever the farmer wanted me to do something, he showed it to me by doing it first. I surely thought the Lutherans would know better than to send German immigrants to an English speaking farmer. We had a language problem and couldn't communicate. He taught me how to drive a tractor and then, somewhat later, would hook up a wagon and put some heavier things on the wagon. The farmer prepared me to drive after him and fill silos. My jobs were to set up the blower, as well as another tractor, and tighten the belt to stay put. The boss went to cut corn in the field, and another farmer would bring the corn to me and blow the cut-up corn into the silo. I learned in a hurry. I saw what the farmer wanted me to do. I had no problem with work. I just could not talk to anyone. Whenever they laughed, I laughed.

I never tasted pies, and these people had different pastries, which I liked. One day my boss showed that on a particular day on the calendar, we were going to a hotel to meet a German man. I understood all that. Therefore, I knew that we were going to meet a German man in a hotel. When we met, the man started to talk. I couldn't understand one word he was saying, because he spoke Pennsylvania Dutch. I was so disappointed because I spoke only High German.

One Sunday, my boss came in to my room and motioned for me to put on my bathing suit—the one he bought for me. We were going for a swim. We drove up to Lake Erie as my boss had a boat and a cottage there. We took off from shore in the boat. I was afraid because I only could see the sky and water. I thought if anyone would want to get rid of a German, he had his chance. My boss stopped the boat until the water was nice and calm, and then he told me to jump in. I was not too sure about it; my boss could see this. He assured me it was okay. I could see that the water was only about three feet deep, so I jumped in. I reached down into the water and brought up something coarse in my hand. I handed it to my boss and he put it into his mouth and said, "Salt." Then I tasted it. It was salt (salz in German). My boss pulled me back into the boat, and we took a wide turn. He pointed out that there was salt everywhere in every direction. Twenty-nine years later, I was a truck driver for a Purina dealer. I had the privilege of going back to that salt mine many times to pick up salt. The salt was sold to many farmers. I got to see the machine that takes the salt out of the water.

While living on the farm, I wrote to Gretel. It had been a few months since we last saw each other. I was glad that Gretel had a good government job in Germany. I just knew that I couldn't uproot her and take her away from her job and family. I didn't want to bring Gretel over to, what? It was not long after that our letters stopped.

In 1951 my sister Rose met a German man. They both came to visit me at the farm. (In time they married and had a daughter they named Rose Marie.) I told them that I had a language problem, so my sister and her friend found me another farm which was just outside of Breslaw where the people spoke some German. Breslaw was on a route to the city of Kitchener where my sister lived. I had to take the Greyhound to their station, and then I took the city bus. I had seen, for the first time in my life, someone read from the Bible and pray at the breakfast table. Even though I didn't understand a word, I felt good about it. At Christmas I spent some time with my boss and some time with my sister. My new boss and his wife gave me socks and underwear. They could see that I had hardly any. They were very good to me.

That year we worked together with Ebby's brother. He had a refugee family living in his other house, and Mike and I worked together for about one year. Mike Gondosch, his wife, mom, dad, and grandparents were living there. They also came from Transylvania but from a different village which I never heard of. Although I was too young to know of that village, we enjoyed each other's company and spoke the same dialect.

Mike's brother was killed on the Russian front in the war. He was in the German army. Mike then married his brother's pregnant wife before the baby was born. This was a fine family. Every time I went to Kitchener, I made a point to see them.

Years later I called the Ottermans just to talk to them and see how they were doing. His wife told me that her husband had lost one arm while harvesting corn while using a blower to blow the corn into a silo (that was my job also). He had to quit farming. Years later, she told me that he had died and that she was living in an old age home in Tilsonburg, Ontario, Canada.

The farmers' wives called each other to inform my boss's wife that they wanted to find a German girl for me. Finally, a call came saying that on the Freeman farm there was a German girl. Mrs. Freeman had just come home from the hospital with newborn twins. My boss told me to hook up a tractor to a wagon, go to the Freeman farm, and pick up something. I knew where the farm was because the boss's wife was from the Hawthorne farm. I had been there several times. The Hawthorne and Freeman farms shared a driveway. I drove there and saw a young girl playing with small children. I introduced myself. Her name was Magdalena Kroh, Lena for short. She had become a refugee from Yugoslavia and ended up in Austria. From there, she immigrated to Elmira, Ontario to be with her sister

Sophie. She found herself a job at the Freeman's farm. In time, I asked her if I could come and visit her after my chores. One evening I rode my boss's bike. On the way home, I had a flat tire. I was about a quarter of a mile from the Freeman's. I thought to go back the way the rear wheel was facing. I then walked back to the farm. Was it ever so dark! I wasn't sure which way to go, so I just took a chance and went back. I knocked on his bedroom window, and I told him what had happened. The kind man drove me home to the farm where I worked. I'm glad I had the flat tire on the bike, as I don't know where I might have ended up! I don't understand why I even thought to drive back home. I was employed. I should have thought dark is dark. I couldn't see my hands in front of my nose! I guess I was eager to see her.

To the left are Maria and standing next to her husband, Leo Kren. To the right of Leo, are Mr. and Mrs. Martin Ruhrig. The man on the left is unknown to me.

On the left are Maria and her husband Leo Kren. She was born in my village; I knew her parents and grandparents. The other couple is Martin Ruhrig, a cousin of Maria, and his wife. Some immigrated to the United States to Youngstown, Ohio; most to Kitchener, Ontario. Years before we all agreed to meet at Niagara Falls. It was good to have seen each other again. We all brought food and shared among ourselves. The men played soccer; I was the goalkeeper. Some stayed in Germany and Austria. I lost track of where everyone was.

Obviously, Lena and I had a lot in common. She got herself a house maid job in the city of Kitchener, for a very nice family who had two little girls. The lady of the house had just come home from the hospital with a little baby boy; today he is a minister. Their family name is Snyder. When I saw that Lena started to put dishes on the table, I left. As I was waiting at the bus stop, a car pulled up. It was driven by the lady of the house. She told me to come into her car. Then she told me that as long as Lena worked for them, by all means, I should stay for supper. I did this maybe twice; I did not want to take advantage of their kindness. After that, I changed the visiting time and went to see Lena in the evenings. On the way home by bus, I fell asleep. I had to walk home which took an hour and a half. I should have told the driver that I wanted to get off at Breslau. Was it ever so dark? No light anywhere! One day I told her that on her day off we would go shopping and that I wanted to buy her a dress. We found one that she really liked. When it came time to pay, I found that I had forgotten that I had bought something earlier and was somewhat short. I felt awful and started to cry. She said, "I am going to buy it."

Here is where I carry Lena, out of love.

Another day she said, "John, you have been in this country for one year and you don't have a car?" Therefore, I went to my boss. Then we went to get my driver's license, and then we went to buy a car. It was an English car. I had to put rocks in the trunk so the car would stay on the road, because the engine was heavier than the body of the car. Our first trip was to Niagara Falls. We had learned about it in school, and now we had a chance to see it in person. We went there often; sometimes we went to Toronto and Hamilton. We had good times.

My lady friend was with me when we came to a crossroad. I used my arm to show I wanted to go left. The officer stopped me and showed me that I had a signal indicator. I never did that again. I didn't know anything about using a turn signal to show which way I wanted to go.

Lena and I.

Lena and I in the year 1951,
one of our first kisses.

The more I was with Lena the more I loved her. God sent her to me. We started to talk about marriage. We were old enough to know what and who we wanted in our lives. I worked on Ebby's farm for a half year longer because they were so good to me. I was paid $600.00 a month.

The most important thing that happened was that I got married on October 11, 1952. This was the happiest day, month, and year of my life. I really loved her. I found that we were good for each other. I kept myself for her until we got married. Our wedding took place in the Lutheran Church in Elmira. The reception was at Lena's sister's house, also in Elmira. We came to the conclusion, as we reminisced about being in Austria as refugees, that we may have been dancing together and that we were meant for each other. I am a blessed man to have had her as my wife.

Our Wedding Day!
The day of our marriage, October 11, 1952. My two sisters,
Sophie on the right and Rose on the left.

My bride Lena with two Snyder girls.

Lena and I dancing together at our wedding reception.

Even after we got married we visited her sister and her husband George and family. We had many rides together to visit other people they knew in different cities. Almost every weekend we were together. George worked in a foundry years later. I started to work there too, as George got me in. I worked there for only one or two years.

My dear sister-in-law, my wife's sister, Sophie, and her husband, George. Behind them is their nice cottage.

As time went by, George and Sophie built themselves a nice cottage close to a lake. My wife, our daughter, and I visited them there. Whenever we could, we drove to Elmira to my wife's sister. One day on the way home after visiting, I must have dozed off and drove for a couple of seconds on the shoulder of the road. I woke up, and my wife asked what I was doing on the shoulder. I said, "A birdie was sitting on the middle of the road." My wife said "Sure, John."

My wife and I had a one-bedroom apartment on the second floor. One day I was off work (I changed shifts), and there was a knock at the door. I went down to see who it was and there stood Martin Schlarp. We both looked at each other and I said, "What are you doing here?" He asked if Magdalena Kroh lived here. I told him, "She is my wife." He took off. My wife told me stories of her cousins who were married to Martin's family. When a mother would nurse a baby, Martin's father would take the baby and give it to an older lady to care for. Then he would tell the mother of the baby to get out and work in the field. I got to know Martin Schlarp when I was working in my first flour mill in Germany. He was also one of those beggars in 1946. (Twenty-eight years later Martin Schlarp came from Toronto to Florida on vacation with some other people. Nothing was mentioned about our past.)

The Bidners.
My sister Sophie on the right, and my other sister Rose on the left.
My sister's husband John is in the middle.

The Bidners built their own house in my neighborhood. My sister and her family lived in their basement until they had enough money to finish it. Finally, it was completed. It was a lovely house. After a while my sister had a breathing problem; her doctor suggested that a climate change may be helpful. So they rode west by train. After they passed the Rocky Mountains on the way to Vancouver, her breathing became easier. So they sold their house in Kitchener and moved to Vancouver. Both worked and their son went to school there.

After a few years their son, Johnny, got married to Mary. They had two boys and one girl. Michelle, John, and David live in British Columbia. David and I are corresponding. Johnny, my nephew, passed on with a heart attack early in his life.

The Bidners' daughter's wedding day. Spring of 2005.

Dave Bidner, the grandson of my second oldest sister,
Sophie. He lives in Prince George, B.C., Canada with his family,
wife Szilvia, and two daughters, Colleen and Stefania.

My nephew John and Mary Bidner with their two boys; later on they had a daughter.

Twenty years later we were invited to Mike Gondosch's daughter's wedding. After the wedding dinner was served and the dishes cleared, two men walked around with beer asking what we wanted to drink. My wife said, "7 Up," and I said, "Me, too." The man said, "Go get it yourself." We sat at the last long table with about seven or eight couples that I knew. When they found out that we were not drinking beer, one couple after another left our table. The latecomers who were not invited to dinner sat at our table. One of the guests, a man, came to me, sat at our table, and asked if I was a Christian. I told him, "Yes." This man was in the German Army. He told me that he feels so bad that he killed so many of our enemies. I told him, "You shouldn't feel guilty about that. The guilt should be on the government that sent you." I know that man felt better because of what I told him. He asked, "Are you sure?" I assured him not to feel guilty.

Our Transylvania custom was to put two chairs at the end of the hall, one for the bride and one for the groom. The announcer would then ask if anyone would like to dance with the bride or the groom. Before you could dance with them, you would have to put some money in the plate on the chair for their honeymoon. We waited until the end because we wanted to justify with the word of God that we should honor people. After the dance, we felt good about it. I like to hear the brass band playing. We had the nicest traditions, and in Kitchener, they still keep them up. I grew up with the brass band and dancing in my village.

My oldest son was born on 4th December, 1953. I wrote to my parents that they were grandparents. We named our son John. No one in our family had middle names, including me. The only one with a middle name was our son, John Frederick Hunyady. His middle name was after Lena's father. My parents passed on between the ages of 65-68 with asthma. I was so sorry that my sister Rose and I could not go to their funeral.

My sister Sofia Bidner's gravestone in Vancouver, B.C., Canada. While my sister and I were in Germany in 1983 to visit my oldest sister and family, my brother-in-law took us to see our dad's grave.

When my wife was in the hospital for my first son, she had another lady with her and one day my wife's doctor came in the room. He said, "Hello, Mrs. Hunyady." After her doctor left, the other lady asked my wife if she really was Mrs. Hunyady. My wife said, "Sure." The other lady asked her, "Do you know how famous your name is?" My wife turned and said with pride, "I'm one of them."

About my dad, I can say, "Thank you for teaching me what I know today. I use every opportunity to be good, kind, understanding, loving, and helpful. I have seen you doing just that to our customers. You always handled yourself very well in different circumstances. I am very proud of you. You are my hero. Looking back, I have never seen you bursting out in anger toward Mom or us. Yes, there were times you may have been disappointed and for that, I understand."

About my mom, "Mom, you showed your character in what you have done for us. We always had clean clothes. You did the best you knew how. For that and for many thousands of reasons, I thank you. You made the best meals. You made good tasty dishes. You liked to make the Romanian dish, mamaliga. It is made out of corn which was taken to the mill and ground into flour. Then it would be made into porridge. I would eat it with warm chocolate milk. I will never forget the good soups you made. I could not have had a better mother than you. I am sorry that Rose and I left you in Germany. It was rough for everyone, young and old. I was hoping that you lived long enough for us to have money so Rose and I could bring you over to us."

My family standing in front of our house.

My second son Karl was born in December of 1955. My wife was hard to persuade that I wanted a girl. She asked, "How could we know if it is going to be a girl?" I said, "We are going to pray her in." My daughter Cindy was then born in November 1962. All three children had middle names. We attended the Lutheran Church.

One day when my little boy came home from kindergarten, he asked me where his mom was. I told him that the ladies in the neighborhood were having coffee in the afternoon. Finally, when she came home, she said to Karl, "You wanted to tell me something?" He said, "I wanted to tell you what I learned today." She said, "Well, Karl, you can tell me now." He thought for a moment and then said, "I forget."

I started to work in a tannery in Kitchener. After two years working there I got word that the company would have some layoffs. I went to look for a different job. I found work in the Electro Porcelain Factory where I worked four shifts.

I had no problem adjusting. I worked there for seven to eight years. I worked with German and Canadian men. There is where I picked up some English. I enjoyed the two dances and good food paid for by the company. The shop union paid for the second dance which they held in the fall. My wife met Frieda Keathler. She lent my wife a record of three men singing from the Mennonite Brethren Church. When I came home from work, she had the record player playing German music. My comment to her was that I liked what I heard. That was the first time I heard gospel music. In fact, I did not even know what it was; I had never heard the word "gospel" before. Frieda invited my wife and me to the Mennonite Brethren Church. That is where we met Peter Dick, Cornelius Wohlgermuth, and other fine people.

Kurt and Frieda Keathler and I.

We were at Frieda's house many times to have coffee or tea. She worked very hard raising three boys and providing a roof over their heads, beds to sleep in and food on the table. She talked a lot about her church and about the Lord. We went home blessed. She told us that the Russians incarcerated her husband Kurt in a Siberian prison because he was a member of the German Army. He spent twenty-five years in that prison. The only communication she had with him was through a family member who lived in Siberia. We all were so happy for Kurt's release. I know many prayers went up for Kurt.

One day Kurt showed up at Frieda's door. The adjustment was difficult for her and the boys. We attended Sunday school at the Mennonite Brethren Church, which we really enjoyed. Here is where my two boys accepted Jesus in their hearts. One day after church we went for a walk. We sat on a bench while Mom prepared our meal. I asked the boys what they had learned in Sunday school. My son Johnny told me that they learned today that a man should work six days, and the seventh is for rest. "How come I worked on Sundays?" "Well, fellas, as you know, we have a nice house just across from the school, we have a mortgage, a roof over our heads, many other things, and the money was good." They pestered me about work on a Sunday. To be a good example, I quit and found myself a six-day job. My boys were happy, and we could also go places.

In 1955, I became a Canadian citizen. I can remember a German man in front of me, and as he stood in front of the judge, he said, "Sir, I was a good German citizen and now that I am in Canada, I will be even a better Canadian citizen." I felt the same way.

We had a spiritual battle. My wife suggested we go to a Bible believing church. I told her that I was brought up as a Lutheran, and I'd stay a Lutheran. One day I asked her if she would be willing to talk to our Lutheran minister. My wife said, "John, anytime."

I asked the Lutheran pastor to come and talk to my wife. I no longer knew how to answer her questions about the Word of God. The pastor, with all his knowledge, didn't even know that we were part of his church. When he came, we sat in a triangle, so that I would be able to hear everything he had to say. My wife fired questions at him; he avoided her questions. He would ask if we were sure that we belonged to his flock. Finally he got up, went to the door and said, "My dear people, don't read too much of the Bible; come more often to church." I was disappointed about what he said. I was shocked to hear that my wife knew so much about the Word of God. This happened on a Friday; my wife asked why I didn't tell her that the minister was coming. I said,

"Do you think I am stupid to tell you, so you can prepare yourself for him?" The following Sunday my wife said, "John, you're the man of the house; which church shall we go to today?" I said that we would go to the Lutheran church. That particular day, the usher seated us in the front row; it was the first time we ever sat so close to the pastor. We were not even ten feet away from the pulpit. I could see that the pastor was nervous that my wife was there. When the time came to read the Epistles he kept looking at my wife as if to say, "If you don't believe me, what are you doing here?" During the sermon, the pastor was at a loss for words. He asked the congregation if someone could repeat his last sentence; that was the last time we attended that Lutheran church.

We would go back there only for weddings and funerals. All in all, I was disappointed that the minister had said we should not read the Bible too much and to come more often to the church. Even I knew that he should have never said that.

We went to the Mennonite Brethren Church for two years. This is where I changed from the Lutheran faith to a Bible believing church on Ottawa Street. This is where I accepted Jesus into my heart; I didn't want to be left behind. Then I knew that I was born again. Then, in 1963, I was baptized as an adult because Jesus' commandment is to follow Him, even in baptism, as Jesus was baptized in the Jordan River. I remember one day, while attending the Mennonite Brethren Church, Ed Funk and I sang tenor; others practiced in every Mennonite Brethren Church all over the district. We all gathered in Eden Christian College. There were about five hundred male singers. We took Frieda with us. I wish that I had bought a tape of our singing. After awhile my good friend Ed Funk died. I heard his younger son sing, "His Eye Is on the Sparrow and I Know He Watches Me."

One day I asked my wife if she knew that she was unequally yoked together with an unbeliever. My wife said that she prayed about that and for me to someday "see the light," in other words, that I would accept Jesus into my heart. As I studied the Bible I learned more and more about the Word of God. When anyone would complain that there were so many different churches and denominations, my wife would simply say, "If the ministers would be closer to the Word of God, there wouldn't be so many churches."

These are a different kind of Mennonite with their only form of transport that they use. They use them in the fields. Here they meet together for church services which are in the vicinity of Elmira, Ontario.

Mike Karst and his wife Lona.

I had a friend, Mike Karst, who had a farm close to Kitchener. He also grew up in Heidendorf, Romania, my village. We had gone to the same school and church. Then in 1944, we all became refugees. We had to flee our country and leave everything behind. At that time we didn't know if we would ever see each other again.

I thought that I might like country living, so Lena and I talked about it. Mike sold his smaller farm and bought about a 200-300 acre farm. Now he was a real dairy farmer. Lena and I went to visit Mike and his wife (who was from Germany). I knew her as a young lady delivering mail in the village where my parents lived. Mike and his wife encouraged us to buy a farm. He would help us with his machinery. I told him that we were going to a different church; it didn't matter to Mike as long as we worked together during the day.

One day Mike called and told me that about four to five km. from his farm, 100 acres was being auctioned off. He kept me informed about the farm that was for sale, and I purchased it. There was no electricity or plumbing in the house. The address of the farm was RR#1 Gowantown in Ontario, Canada. In October 1963, we moved to the farm because I did not want to pay rent in the city. Before I bought the farm, I had to sell my three-bedroom house. The two boys went to school. That winter we had our honeymoon, which we never had before. My wife and I had our bedroom downstairs close to the road. We could hear anyone coming up the lane to the house. Our children had their bedroom upstairs. Mike Karst bought slabs of wood for our stove. We had to burn it day and night.

Our Farm.

My daughter Cindy and my grandson Michael.

My family on the farm next to our car.

Almost every evening we were at the Karst farm talking a lot about farming and enjoying each other's company. We had my little girl with us. We were at the time attending a Mennonite Brethren church. And one night they said that if we didn't come to their church, our friendship was over. My wife said to me, "Well John, we have nothing to do here." At the door, my wife said, "Mike and Lona, you can be mad at us all you want. John and I will leave your house in peace." With that we left. And once we started farming, we were so busy with farm work that we did not see the Karsts for many years except at weddings or funerals.

That winter the boys each had a toy tool. One had an ax and the other had a small saw. One day we went in our forest to look for a Christmas tree. (I had the real saw.) The snow was deep to walk in, so I carried my daughter. I said to the boys, "Before we cut, let us all agree on a tree." I asked Cindy, "Do you think this tree is good enough for our Christmas tree?" All she said was, "OK." She was bundled up. Therefore, we all agreed on that tree. Next, we had to pull it home on the snow. We set it up in the living room for the next day where my wife and Cindy would decorate it. That night it snowed, and in the morning we had snow as high as three feet in the living room. That did not happen the next winter, because I put new siding on the house.

My son John and another boy went to the same school. During the following spring my son brought home a note from his friend's father. As my wife and I drove in, he took us in his house and wanted to apologize for pushing up the price of the farm because he didn't know whether we were just investing or wanted to become a home-owner. I thanked him for being so honest and telling us. He had wanted the land for himself, as he had it leased and was not sure for how long. Well, we shook hands; then he gave us a gallon of fresh maple syrup for free. He offered God's blessing on our endeavor.

I remember my friend had warned me that there would be times on the farm that we would not have any food on the table for our family, because my income would have to go to the ones I owed money. I thank God that that never happened. We always had something to eat. I loved the soups my wife would make from the vegetables in the garden; she would throw in a few from every available kind of vegetable along with the meat. She knew how, even as a young girl, to improvise very well. She went through the war and was a refugee. Therefore, she knew how to survive.

There were four or five other farmers on a phone party line. We each had our own ring. One day my wife went to the grocery store to buy our supplies, and she asked a lady in the store if she knew where a certain item was. The lady answered by asking, "Are you the one who bought the Kroft's farm?" My wife told her, "Yes." She came home and told me the story, and we surmised that this lady must have been listening in on our telephone conversations for her to recognize my wife's voice.

One day a man from the Mennonite Brethren Church came to visit us. He saw that we didn't have any electricity. I told him that we wouldn't have any money to pay him. He told us that he would install the hardware that would give us electricity, at no cost to us. After two weekends, we had electricity. I was very grateful to Peter Dick that he came and installed electricity in our farm house. But I feel awful that I did not give him first chance to install electric throughout the house and barn. Our garden produced an abundance of vegetables, so I gave this kind man all kinds of vegetables that summer.

Many times, we drove past a small country church. We were looking for a large church like the Mennonite Brethren Church, but we couldn't find one. Then one Sunday we stopped in. The usher was Harold Srigley. He had two daughters who sang many times in the church; their mother played the piano. They sang songs like "Jesus Loves Me," "This Little Light of Mine," and others. In this country church the congregants were all farmers, about 40–45 people, young and old. They were very friendly.

My wife fell in love with this little country church.

My wife and I after coming home from the country church.

In the winter at church we had a pot belly stove; the children sat close to it to keep warm. In this church, I met John Johnson, Lloyd Faust, and other fine people. The same minister had two charges; when we had our Sunday school, Palmerston church had their church service, and the pastor was there. After the service, he came to us for our church service. About one year later, one Sunday, the minister said that General MacArthur gathered his men, and he prayed for the Lord to help them fight the enemies (the enemies were the Germans). The minister must have forgotten that he had a German family in the church at the time. My wife and I looked at each other and we held hands. From that day on, my boys never went to church. The boys said that the minister should never have said that. We went to Sunday school and church.

In time, our country church was sold to a Mennonite group. When the country church dissolved, some people went to the Listowel sister church. Others, however, went to the other sister church in Palmerston. Although my boys did not come, my wife, daughter and I did go to the Palmerston Missionary Church. We attended Sunday school first and then church service with my daughter.

One day my wife Lena sent me to Harriston to buy some meat. I saw Harold there. We sat in the car and talked for about two hours. I told Harold I had no knowledge about farming because I was relying on my good friend. Harold told me that he would help. Then one day, when the fields were dry enough to walk on, Harold drove in. He checked what each field needed and numbered every field. We talked and he gave me instructions on what seeds and fertilizers to buy.

In the winter of 1963, Harold drove his tractor and plowed the snow off our lane so we could attend the country church. My Cindy would stand at the kitchen window all dressed up. As soon as she would see Harold driving in, she would shout out, "Here comes our angel."

After I got the seed and fertilizer, one Saturday seven to eight tractors drove in, each with different implements. In just one day whatever needed to be done on our hundred acre farm was done. The farmers' wives helped make sandwiches, and we were so thankful! After everything was sown, in a couple of weeks, depending on the weather, we could see sprouting start, and slowly the rows were forming. My wife and I dropped to our knees thanking God for allowing us to buy the farm and praying for the good Lord to help us in every way, in Jesus' name. I could not wait to see things sprout. I would scratch the earth away just to see how things were coming up. One of my neighbors had a combine, and I was grateful when I had my harvest in. Then it was time for the fall work. For years Harold and I helped each other with our farm work.

My sister Rose, the Srigleys, and the Fausts.

Harold and his wife Winnie Srigley invited us to go with them to a full gospel fellowship international for breakfast. My wife and I took them up on this. The chapter meeting was at the Blue Barn at that time. The speaker was Benny Hinn; the year was 1964. Today, it is called the Country Inn in Listowel. We enjoyed the meeting. I heard for the first time that they believe the Bible from cover to cover. I had never heard this before; we went home blessed. My wife grew up in a full gospel church in Yugoslavia. It is always good to hear the gospel no matter how old a person is. The older I get, the sweeter Jesus becomes. Every time we went to another chapter meeting, I enjoyed it more. As time went by, I joined them, but before joining, I wanted to be baptized in the Holy Spirit. This chapter voted me to be their head usher; therefore, no matter how busy I was on the farm, I was always ready to go to the full gospel meetings. Harold always said that tomorrow is another day. Even if it would rain, Harold would say, "The One that makes it wet will make it dry."

I have gone through many countries and met many men, but no one comes close to this man. I remember the day I saw him the second time. We started talking. He was so sensitive that he knew I wanted to talk to him. I felt he wanted to get to know me. He asked questions about my past. I told him as much as I could, that I was born as a Lutheran. I married a fine lady who knew the Lord. I just had accepted Jesus into my heart and we were attending a Mennonite Brethren church. Then we felt led to buy a farm. I told him I was shocked that my friend Mike and I were both born in the same village. Then Mike told me that we could work together; in fact he said I should give more money down for the farm. Mike would use his machinery to help me out, so that I wouldn't have to buy a tractor. I was a greenhorn when it came to farming. I told all of this to this kind man. Then he said that he would help me. I was so happy when I came home to my wife and told her. We thanked the Lord that He led me to meet a man that would help us. We worked very well together. We complemented each other.

Harold took me under his wings. As members of the chapter, we were encouraged to visit other chapters. One evening I went to another chapter meeting in Stratfort. The meals were good, as always, and worship was great. The speaker came on. He spoke much about the past (many people tried to forget). He spoke about how the Nazis came and took his father, and he never saw him again. That happened to so many thousands of our people. Well, let me tell you, not only were the Jews taken away. So were the Germans by the millions. I read in a small booklet that in Yugoslavia the Germans were all gathered to a place where they had to dig deep holes. I'm not sure how deep. They all had to stand at the edge of that hole. Then the machine gunners shot every one of them. They poured lime over the bodies and then a bulldozer covered them all. At the end of that hole was a young boy who was only wounded. He grew to be a mature young man who published everything. It says that other countries were involved in this. So not only have the Jews suffered, there were millions of Germans killed. My wife brought it with her from Yugoslavia, Serbian. That happened to so many thousands of our people. I never saw them again, either.

I was sitting in the middle of the aisle; I could not leave because I knew many chapter members. When I got home, in time, I called the President of my chapter and told him about this man. He told me that he had booked him two months ago. When the man came to speak in our chapter, I did what I had to do. When he came to the pulpit, I excused myself, because I did not want to hear the same message again. I went to the door ready to go out when I heard him speak of the love of God, that He shed His blood on the Cross of Calvary for the sins of the world. Dying on the Cross of Calvary, He was buried in a tomb, and three days later, Jesus arose from the dead. He lives in our hearts. This man had a more profound message. The whole time he was speaking, I was sitting on the edge of my chair. After a half an hour of preaching, he gave an invitation to go to a different room where he would come speak to us. This man spoke some more and prayed for me to receive the baptism of the Holy Spirit. While he prayed for me, I started to speak in the Romanian language. He told me not to speak the Romanian language. (I thought I forgot it.) Then he prayed some more, and I spoke the heavenly language with boldness. I went home blessed knowing that I had received something that I know many other people would like to have. From that time on, I continued to seek out full gospel churches, even up until this very day.

My wife had a cousin living in Toronto. He and his wife would come out to the farm at least three to four times a year to visit. I said grace then, and this man told us that he doesn't believe in this "Jesus Christ stuff." One day his wife called to inform us that her husband had passed on. My son and Debby were always willing to help us out with our chores. At the funeral I waited until the last, and I stood next to his casket, knowing he could not answer me, and asked, "Where are you going to spend your eternity?"

In the summer of 1964, we bought cattle and started to ship milk by cans. About half a year later the Milk Marketing Board encouraged every dairy farmer to switch over to bulk in one to two months.

I am driving a tractor with milk cans.

We tried to keep up the quality of the milk. I had a herd of Jersey cows like those that Mike had. I found out that these cows' production was high in butterfat. The Jersey Association sent us a catalog stating that if we needed to buy or sell, call the number that was in the catalog. My son called a farmer who told him that he had a promising bull that was free. At the time, we had a Volkswagen car. We took the back seat out of the car, put many burlap bags on the floor, and went to see the calf. It was free all right. We loaded the calf and tied his hind legs together. By the time we arrived home about an hour and a half later, you can only imagine the way the bull smelled, and we all stunk! I told my son that it was his idea. P.S. I never thought in my life that I would have an animal in my car. My son told me that he would clean the car. I am not sure if I helped. In the car were my wife, my daughter, my son and, of course, the bull calf. Some Jersey farmers and I had a hard time raising the Jersey calves. Very slowly, I switched over to Holstein cows. These calves were able to endure a little draft. I renovated the stalls making them wider and longer.

I am very glad that I had a wife. Whenever I went out in the middle of the night to check on a cow, I told her if I was not back in five minutes to come out, rain or shine, to check on me.

The beginning of farming was very hard. Soon, our money ran out; therefore, my wife and I had to return to work. We took turns milking in order to go to work because we only had one vehicle. She worked at night for Campbell's Soup, and I worked at Spin Rite. I always enjoyed whistling. If I whistled a gospel song, I could find out if anyone in the plant was a Christian. One day a minister came over and told me that he liked the song I was whistling. We had a chance to talk; I found out he had a church. My wife and I went to hear him. He told me that his denomination did not believe that a minister should be paid by his flock. At Spin Rite, one day while on my break, I was sitting outside drinking water, and one man asked me about the union. All I said was, "I never worked for a company that had a union, so I cannot tell you." When I made that statement about the union, a man from the office walked by and overheard me say "union." Before leaving for home, I was called into the office, and they told me, "Today is your last day." They asked why I was talking about the union. I told them the same thing that I told the first gentleman, that I did not know anything about it. I would have been more satisfied if the office asked the man to whom I had just spoken.

My daughter enjoyed playing at the water pump. She was always wet. I made sure that the planks were strong enough as the years went by. One day she saw that her younger brother beat the older one, but sometime later she fought both of them and won. She happily showed off with the victory sign.

My daughter Cindy at the water pump.

My sons; Karl beats up Johnny, while Cindy looks on.

Cindy beat both boys and raised her arms up in victory.

My son Johnny with our Jersey Heifer at 4-H.

My oldest son started to go to a 4-H Club to learn about farming. (Later he became one of their leaders.) In time he knew the difference between a regular cow and a purebred. Slowly he encouraged me into those kinds of cows. Our son got more and more involved with showing other farmers' cows and calves at country fairs. He won many showmanship ribbons. We went to see him sometimes at the fairs, and we were very proud of him

Johnny got his driver's license. One day the school had a dance, and my son asked to borrow our car. He picked up a farmer boy in the neighborhood and my other son, Karl. On his way home my son realized that he had forgotten the other boy, and he drove back to pick him up. This boy lived on a gravel road. My son must have been speeding, for as he turned left to his friend's farm, he went too fast and was unable to stop. The car flew into the air and landed on top of a big slab of cement from an old bridge. The car rested there. The boy's father must have been waiting for him. He must have heard the impact. He came to check things out and found his son in the car bleeding. He rushed him to the hospital. The son had to have a few stitches. My neighbors drove by the place of the accident, and they saw my two boys in the car. They rushed to my house and came into my bedroom at about 1 A.M. or 2 A.M. and told us what they saw. We rushed to the scene of the accident. Johnny was okay, but we drove Karl to the hospital where he had to have stitches.

I remember my daughter Cindy and the boys had a long walk to the house. We had a goose that started to play with my Cindy every time she came home. The goose would meet her, and as time went by, I saw that the goose pecked Cindy on her cheek. I told my wife that I didn't like that because the goose might go for her eyes, although she wore glasses. I suggested to my wife that we kill the goose and eat it. Later on, at dinner, Cindy said, "Boy, this is a big bird. Oh, by the way, has anyone seen the goose?" We just looked at each other. Cindy said, "No! You didn't!" I nodded. She ran out of the house crying, and I tried to tell her, "I saw the goose peck on your cheek and next would be your eyes." Slowly, she agreed, but she still wouldn't eat any more of the bird. One day I surprised her with a pony, and she promised me that she would feed and water her and ride her. This went on for a couple of weeks. Then I saw that Cindy neglected the pony. I confronted her, and she said that she had so much homework to do. I told her that I would take it to the stockyard. Well, she didn't help with the pony. I sold it. Cindy cried for her pony. I told her that I gave her a chance.

A couple named Kurt and Frieda from the Mennonite Brethren Church came to visit us on the farm. They brought with them a little girl from their neighborhood. We all had a good time. Before they left, my wife gave them a gallon of fresh milk out of the bulk tank which was nice and cold. When they arrived home, the woman asked the girl if she would like a glass of fresh milk right from the cows. The little girl said, "No, thank you. I only drink milk from the milkman."

I just loved to walk beside a field of grain, touching here and there a stalk of grain just to see how it was growing. Then I walked through the cornfield. I could see that every week the corn grew. After a while, it grew much taller than me. I've tried not to have many weeds in my cornfield because it spoils the quality of feed for my cows. That was my pride and joy.

My brother-in-law, Martin, always wanted to help out by driving a tractor. I hooked up a harrow behind the tractor. Rosemary stood next to her dad. We had a cookout by having bacon on a long stick hanging over the fire. Toasted bread was dunked into the grease. It was so good.

My brother-in-law Martin with his daughter Rosemarie, my niece.

Here is my family at Rose Marie Poschner's confirmation.

In time, Frieda became ill. Sometime later, she went to be with the Lord. May she rest in peace. It was a big loss for her family and church and people who knew her. Years later, I called Kurt at his house. A woman by the name of Wanda answered and told me that she was Kurt's wife. She told me that Kurt had a stroke and was in the Kitchener Waterloo Hospital. After he came home, I called a couple of times

One day, my boys came home from school and one of them asked Mom if the Germans were really that bad? My wife and I just looked at each other. No matter what my wife would have said, our boys would sooner believe their teacher because he had the biggest influence on them. My wife simply said to the boys that they should never forget that there are good and bad people all over the world. One of them said that made sense.

One rainy day, my wife and I took the opportunity to go shopping for shoes for my oldest son, Johnny. As we walked to the store, my wife and I were conversing in German. Johnny was about ten feet in front of us. He stopped in his tracks and said, "Will you speak English?" My wife put one finger on her lips and said, "As long as these lips are alive, they will speak German, whether you like it or not." Whenever we were in an English speaking circle, we adjusted ourselves, and we spoke English the best we knew how. I am still learning.

My children did well in school. Cindy helped where she could. Karl, our youngest son, also helped with the chores on the farm. He loved working with the tractor at night. Karl said that I should prepare the tractor and an implement. I was able to purchase my neighbor's 138 acre farm with a barn. I was also a pig farmer. I had so many sows and little pigs running around! I kept the litters from birth to slaughter. My neighboring farmer was Harold Srigly's father-in-law. He operated 150 acres. His name was Shoemaker. We helped each other out, especially in harvest time. We only had so much time to do our harvest. This man came and showed me how to castrate the male pigs. I kept all the females. I felt sorry for them at first, but I knew it had to be done. I remember one year on the farm in the winter putting many burlap bags on my kitchen floor close to the stove, which burned 24 hours. There I kept the little piglets and calves that needed special attention. They all needed the extra warmth. At that time, if I could, I would have had them in my bed between my wife and me, but she would not let me. I had a low fat-producing cow; the children fed milk to my little herd in the house before going to school, until the animals were strong enough to put in another pen in the barn.

These pictures were taken on the farm; Lena and me, Cindy and me, and Lena and Cindy.

My lovely wife, Lena, of twenty-eight years; she was not afraid of anything.

My little girl Cindy poses for a picture with her dad.

My two loveliest ladies in the whole wide world, my wife Lena and daughter Cindy.

In the main barn, I installed a stable cleaner. Later I installed a 20' x 70' silo with an unloader. I enjoyed being able to buy a new tractor, and plow at a plowing match in the winter. We would all use that tractor as a means to get to church in winter time. One year at the plowing match a heavy rain came and people lost their shoes in the mud. A truck filled with many sizes of rubber boots came around. The owner sold them all. There still were people who walked in their socks. I always had a pair of rubber boots in my pickup truck; I learned to come prepared.

One day I bought fifteen purebred cows, and five of them had to be slaughtered for various reasons. My brother-in-law warned me about a board being weak on the wooden bridge. I assured him that I would replace it. Sure enough, my cows went over the bridge to the pasture. On the way back, one of the cows stepped on the board, fell through and broke her right leg. I called my neighbor Don Gedke, and he came over with his tractor and rope. He had to drive down in the creek, but there was not much water. I tied the rope behind the front legs of the cow and Don lifted her out. We laid her on my three-quarter ton pickup truck. I did a mercy killing because she was suffering. Then I drove her to the butcher. The meat was good. My wife was angry with me. I said to her, "If you saw me doing something wrong, why didn't you tell me?"

I had many dogs on my farm. One day a new calf was born. At first they wobble around, but once they start running, there is no stopping them. My daughter went to the calf, and the calf sucked Cindy's fingers. Then all of a sudden the calf's mother with horns charged my daughter. I was only two to three feet behind her. I just couldn't get her away. All of a sudden my dog ran and jumped on the cow's head long enough for me to rescue Cindy. My dog had steaks for his job well done!

I had another big heavy cow. According to her papers, she came from good stock. I paid extra money for her. I knew that she would soon give birth. One day I cleaned out the pig manure in the pen. I washed and disinfected that pen, and when good and dry, I put lots of straw in there. I let the cow in and kept my eyes on her. It just happened that I was there when she wanted to get up. Her legs slipped sideways, and she fell on her belly. I called the vet. Tom came and said, "I could kick your pants. Why didn't you leave the pig manure in there? She would have had much better footing." I said that I meant well, to have a nice big clean pen. By her fall, she broke her back. I called the butcher, and he came and killed her. I pulled her out with my tractor, loaded her up with my manure fork lift, and put her on my pickup truck. I drove her to the butcher's shop. The meat was good.

My family on the farm.

Cindy is holding my granddaughter Karin, and
my grandson Michael is leaning on the chair.

No matter how busy we were on the farm we always made a point to get up one hour earlier on Sunday in order to get all our chores done before leaving for church. We tried to milk the cows in twelve hour intervals. We went first to Sunday school and then to the church service. My wife and I had our differences.

We had our Bibles between us until one Sunday the minister said, "We're going to sing 'God Will Take Care of You.'" My wife and I looked at each other. We took our Bibles from between us, came closer together, and held hands as the congregation sang "God Will Take Care of You." A healing took place. From that day on, those five cows were never mentioned again. We still had to make payments on them, but soon we didn't feel the crunch anymore because the other cows were a blessing.

One night I went out to check on a Jersey cow. I saw her head down on the straw. This was not a good sign, so I sat down next to her and put her head in my lap. When my wife came out, I asked her to call the vet. He came at 1:00 A.M. The vet did all he could do, but he couldn't help her anymore; she died on my lap. I had a Jewish dealer coming in. We always spoke German. He asked if I had any cows to cull (free boarders). Sometimes I did and sometimes I did not.

I had a $1,500 cow. I made sure I went out to her at least every hour. The last visit to her was 5:15 A.M. My wife and I went in to start chores at 5:45 A.M. While she started milking by machine, I went to check on this particular cow. I found her dead. She had given me a little heifer calf. She pushed so hard to clean herself, she pushed out her womb. After that I knew how a womb looked. At the same time, I checked on another cow; she was not ready to give birth. I saw that she had pushed out about two to three inches of her womb. It was a puzzle to me. I washed my hands in her water to clean them. I kept my hands under the tail. My wife came. She called the vet. Vet Tom came and he put two wooden pins through the cow's female organs. Tom said that after ten days I could pull the upper pin out and leave the other for a few more days after she gave birth. After three months, once she was in calf I sold her.

At one point, I could not pay the feed bill. One day the manager of the feed mill came to collect the bill, and, again, I told him that I did not have the money to pay. He then asked to go to the front field. There were approximately twenty-five acres of grain to be harvested. This grain would normally be used to feed my cattle. The manager asked me when it would be ready for harvest. I told him in a week or ten days. He told me to call him then, and he would send his trucks to pick up the grain. I had my own combine. He would use the proceeds from this grain to pay my feed bill. My wife and I went in the granary to check things out and saw that we would not have enough grain to feed all the cattle and pigs. We held hands, cried, and prayed that the Lord would stretch the grain. When spring came I had enough to use some of the grain for seed grain. Sometime later, I received a check for $5,000. It was for the excess grain that the manager of the feed mill took. With this money, I bought a small feed mill. I installed it myself. It gave me the capacity to make my own chop.

I had a smaller combine than this one on the farm.

Years later, my wife took my hands into hers and told me that she was going to die. That she was sorry for things she did and did not do, and for things she said and didn't say. I said, "What are you talking about? I am older than you and would go first." She said, "No, not this time around." She told me that when she died, she wanted the trio from our church to sing "God Will Take Care of You." She also wanted to be buried in the cemetery of the country church that she fell in love with. In time, Cindy my daughter found out that Mommy is going to die. One night there was a knock on the door at about 2:00 A.M. It was Cindy. I asked her, "What is the matter?" She said that she could not sleep because she was thinking about Mommy. Cindy asked, "What is going to happen to me when you die?" By then we had her between us nice and warm. My wife replied to Cindy not to worry because, "Dad will look for a woman that he will make sure she loves you more." Cindy looked at me and asked, "Is that true,

77

daddy?" I said, "By all means, honey." We kept her with us the rest of the night to comfort her. Cindy was about fourteen years old.

My second son Karl got his driver's license. He started working in Listowel, Ontario. One day he got to know another boy at work. The young boy didn't have a ride home, so my son drove him home. Then he realized that he had forgotten that his mom was waiting for him to come home so she could drive to work. He decided it was too slow driving on the road, so he drove in the ditch for a long stretch. But he couldn't stop; he ended up in a culvert. He was taken to the hospital where the doctor used a wire from one temple to the other to keep his head together. He couldn't talk.

Later my son John and his family moved to the farm. We all ate at the same table. I told them that I could not pay them any wages, but to come to me whenever they needed a dollar. They also had free gas for their use, so one day my daughter-in-law came to me in the barn and reminded me of what I had said. She told me that our 25th Wedding Anniversary was coming up, and she wanted to buy us something. She also said that our family would grow, and we would need things. I asked her how much she would need, and she didn't know. Then I sent her in the house to get my checkbook. I gave her a blank check with my signature on it and told her to go buy whatever she needed. She bought two sets of six dishes. To this day, my son has one set and I have the other.

My son Johnny and his family; wife Debbie, Michael, and their daughter Karin

My granddaughter Karin being fed by her Grandma Illman.

I had installed the plumbing in the house, and other people installed the septic tank. I got some new help on the farm. I was always the first one in the barn and the last to leave. That arrangement did not work out.

One day while I did my paperwork, my wife was in her garden as always. She came in and told me that clouds were forming to the west over the Gedkes farm. All I could say was "Keep an eye on them." Twenty minutes later, she said that I should come out and look at them because lightning started. It was about 3:30 P.M. I asked her to wait about another 15 minutes. Sure enough, it was time to bring the cows in for milking. Once lightning started, we would never know if it would hit the main transformer. Speaking of transformers, I changed three transformers in my lifetime on the farm. It did happen that the transformer blew out, so we had to wait until it came on again. That was when I didn't know better. Harold showed me how to use the tractor's airline to milk one cow at a time. Therefore, when it happened, I did the same. My wife would milk two cows while I milked one. We had a lantern in the barn. As time went by, I learned that whenever bad weather was approaching, I should bring the cows in while I had electricity. I learned in a hurry. Many farmers would be without power when a storm hit. Some farmers had generators. It was a good thing when we renovated our barn. I bought bigger surge pumps. We could hook up five milkers if needed, but we never did. My wife milked with two milkers. I brought down as much silage as I thought necessary.

My daughter Cindy walked in early because the school bus brought the children home sooner due to the storm. She asked what she could do. I asked her to prepare water to wash the milkers. The lightning became more severe. All of a sudden, this lightning was too close for comfort. I was in the furthest corner of the barn by the silo. I thought of Cindy having her hands in the water. I ran in the milk house. Lena asked me why I was running. I told her I would tell her later. Cindy just pulled her hands out of the water and said, "Daddy, I can't move my hands." In such a case, I would usually call Harold to come and pray for her, but he was in the same situation as I was. He also had to do the chores like milking and feeding; he too was depending on the electricity. I just couldn't bother him. Therefore, I "took the bull by the horns." I told Cindy to put her hands on top of mine. I placed my right hand on top of hers and started to pray. After a couple of minutes of praying in the name of Jesus, Cindy told me that she could move her little finger. I encouraged her to just keep it up. By that time, I lifted my right hand towards heaven to pray more. Then she pulled one hand after the other off of my hand; she felt okay. All I could say was, "Thank you, Jesus, for healing my daughter's hands."

I was so happy that I had my three sisters with their husbands together in Waterloo at my sister Rose's house. I had not seen my oldest sister and her husband for about fifty years.

The Rauch's wedding. My wife's sister Sophie and her husband George from Elmira, my wife and I.

While on the farm we were invited to Ottawa to my wife's niece's wedding. The Pleins, my wife's sister Sophie and her husband George rode together. We had a good time. My son and his wife Debbie came to help us out while we were gone for a couple of days.

My wife Lena and me from our farm (first row), along with from Germany my oldest
sister Maria (next to me) and her husband John Zautner (behind me), my second oldest
sister Sophie and her husband John Bidner from Vancouver (next to Maria), and my
third oldest sister Rose and her husband Martin Poschner (top row).

My wife's older sister with her family of ten or twelve immigrated to Brazil. The government told them they would help them uproot forest by the acre. They would supply them with fertilizer and seed. They fared well after their retirement. While they lived on the farm in Brazil, they also had small children. Their mom sent the one that was seven or eight years old to do the ironing in the basement. This little girl was curious about the socket. It was then that she put her hairpin in the socket and got electrocuted and died. They had family and friends living there. When we had our farm, they came and visited us for three or four weeks. They enjoyed drinking milk right from the cows that she milked. This couple had one daughter who married a man from Ottawa. Before their daughter got married she came to visit us on the farm. We always enjoyed having her.

Next to my tractor is my family with a new calf and my wife's cousin from Florida.

**My wife's two oldest sisters and their husbands. Standing next to my wife is Cindy.
In the back row are, from right to left, my daughter-in-law Debbie,
my son Johnny, and Cristian.**

In addition to cows, I had many sows on the farm. They would come in (give birth). Sometimes the sows pushed too hard, and therefore the baby piglets were still in the womb. Many times I was there to help. When in a farrowing crate, a sow cannot turn around. She has room to lie down. Crates are good because the sows are in there until after the birth, usually two or three days. A while ago, I read that it is called animal cruelty to have a sow or animal in a cage. It was only for the sow and her newborn's good, and for the farmer, as it saves him money. I was there to guide the little ones to their mother to suck until they opened up their eyes and could find their mother. If piglets wander off, the other sows just push them away with their snout.

One of my sows on my hog farm.

My son Karl wanted to work on the land at night. I kept an eye on him. If he stopped longer than seven to ten minutes I would hop in the car or pickup truck. I wanted to know if he had a problem.

Sometimes we had problems loading up our hogs for the market. On Thursdays, farmers could take their cattle to the stockyard, which was about 60 miles to Kitchener, then five miles east. One Thursday we wanted to load up our hogs, as they were ready for the butcher. We set up our chute walkway for the hogs to go up and get on the truck. This was the normal way, but not with these hogs! They came back, so we had our hands full with the loading. By God's providence our good friend Harold came just in time. How did he know that we had problems? He knew Thursdays was a day for the market and thought maybe we could use some extra help. Well, he kept the pigs from returning and got them up on the truck. I told Harold how thoughtful he was and how much I appreciated it.

One day, my daughter Cindy got her learner's permit. I asked her if she would like to learn how to drive a tractor forward and backwards. Once Cindy learned how to drive the tractor, I then let her drive my car. I trained her to back up between two straw bales. I moved the straw bales closer and closer without her knowing. One Sunday I asked her if she would like to drive the car on the road to the church. I told her that she could drive only about ten miles. When we got to the highway, she wanted to change seats. I said that I was satisfied with her driving; therefore, I would let her drive on the highway. She said, "Daddy!" All I said to her was "Cindy, just drive." She parked the car just right in the church parking lot, and then

I took and kept the keys. Cindy was so happy that I let her drive on the highway. She said, "Thank you Daddy, I love you."

My son Karl always wanted to become a lawyer like Perry Mason. One day he asked me if I could help him. How could I say no? Therefore, I promised him that I would. My mind went one hundred miles an hour on how I was going to pay for his education. There were 300 acres in my neighborhood for sale. I could buy the land and then lease it to other farmers. I would then be able to help my son. One day Karl said that he wanted to try city life. We had warned him not to go with the wrong crowd. While there, he got into the wrong crowd and was caught stealing hubcaps. All his friends left him. Karl ended up in jail near Toronto, Ontario. Instead of going to church, which my wife and I always enjoyed, we drove to see our son. My wife would always ask him why he stole. One day I told him that the banker called me in and asked me why I could not control my son. The banker put a hold on the loans because of the situation with our son. After a few times visiting Karl, he took our heads together and quoted a scripture from the Bible, "Train up a child in the way that he should go, and when he grows old, he shall not depart from it." My wife and I drove home happy knowing that he did not lose his faith in the Lord Jesus Christ.

My second oldest son Karl. He liked to work driving the tractor at night time.

In five years, between my two sons and my daughter-in-law, they wrecked three cars. My wife went to the doctor for her yearly physical. She came home and told me that she had made an appointment for us to see the doctor for the results of his findings. We went to see the doctor, and he said Lena's fifth vertebra was deteriorated and I was to keep her out of the barn. Her working days were over. I asked him about an operation. The doctor asked me if I wanted to push her in a wheelchair for the rest of her life. Of course, I said, "No." "Well, then, keep her out of the barn," he said.

After my wife couldn't help with milking any more, I was looking for a herdsman. One day a lady called saying that she was familiar with dairy farms. I asked her to come to see me. As soon as I saw her, I said to my wife that I don't want her because she was too fragile (skinny). We discussed that her job would be milking, breeding, cleaning, feeding, and helping where needed. I talked her out of the job. I could not discriminate. All I said was that I thought a milker with 50 lbs. would be too heavy for her and that I wouldn't want to take a chance. She left. One or two weeks later I called her and found out that she already had a job on a horse farm. All I can say is that I lost out on her. My wife said, "You going to the barn with another woman, talking about feeding, breeding …" She was just teasing.

A storm came with high winds, and the barn doors were open. I heard them banging against the barn wall. They were open because I had just put in new bales of hay to air them out. I thought I would spread salt over every row of the bales to help prevent heating up. This is why I air dried them. I woke up my wife, and we looked at the clock. It was 2:00 A.M. and raining. We had no choice but to go out there to close those doors. I took my tractor with a manure forklift. My wife and I tried at least three quarters of an hour to fight the wind. I could not have done it alone. Finally, we were able to close the barn doors. I left the tractor with the forklift propped against the doors. We went in the house, washed ourselves and went to bed.

As I said before that we worked together with the Srigleys. One day my wife and I were in the haymow. I had a long elevator that reached one level of the barn. At one time my daughter came home from school. There was no one in the house, so she came to the barn. She heard us talking up in the haymow; all of a sudden I saw that she had come up the elevator to us! I took a hold of her.

One day I cut about 20-25 acres of grass after two or three hot days. Harold and I baled them, and then I stacked them. I left them out for another three days to dry, but instead it started to rain and they became soaked. Once the land started to dry out, one could drive on the land with a tractor. I consulted my good friend Harold about what I should do, and he suggested that I put the match to them. I lost hundreds of bales of hay that year; I was counting on them. I still made it, in spite of the mishap. There was nothing I could have done to prevent this from happening.

While living on the farms, we had many dogs. Once I got a German Shepherd dog, and she had six puppies. One day we came home from our country church and just as we settled down for lunch, a man in a pickup truck drove in. He informed me that my new bunch of dogs had torn up a brand new baby calf. As my litter of six dogs came home, I shot every single one of them. I should have kept their mother, as I could have spayed her, but instead I killed them all. I drove to the owner of the calf and I offered him any animal in my herd. That kind man didn't want any part of that. I told him how sorry I was, and we shook hands in peace.

The reason why I killed all of them is that I found out once dogs have a taste for fresh blood meat, they may do it again. I wanted to prevent them from attacking my own newborn purebred calves.

Sometimes I was so tired, that I would fall asleep at the dinner table, even with food in my mouth. In my left hand I had my fork, with the knife on my right. My wife often said that I should be careful, because one of these days I would poke my eyes out.

By now I had two hundred and thirty-eight acres of land and a nice purebred Holstein herd. Now that my right hand, my wife, couldn't help me anymore, I had to start chores at 5:00 A.M. Breakfast was at 10:00 A.M. Even with all the gadgets, like a stable cleaner and a 20 by 70 foot silo with an unloader, it still took me hours to milk up to fifty cows. Everyday, I had to feed the calves, clean their pens and prepare for their next feeding. So I had no choice; in spite of my best endeavors, I had to think about giving up farming. I was surely hoping that my son would come home to help me, and, in time, he would have helped himself to the farm.

I had a Jersey cow ready to give birth. Meanwhile I played with her udder, trying to get her used to me. I found out that she was ticklish, and then she kicked me on my left knee. I tied her right leg on a post, so it would be harder for her to kick. One day I put my milkers on her. I knew that she had good butterfat milk. All of a sudden she jumped; the milker fell off the belt and spilled her milk. Well, in time, I bred her. When I knew that she was pregnant, I sold her. As a result of that kick, I had many doctor's visits. Every time I walked into the waiting room, no matter how many people were there, as soon as the nurse saw me she called out my name to come to her. The she gave me a cortisone shot right underneath my kneecap.

In December of 1975, my wife's and my heart were broken when we saw all our purebred cattle and hogs being sold. I had to be hospitalized for a knee operation. While in the hospital, my wife and my only daughter celebrated Jesus' birth. My wife brought good food and wine. I shared it with them. We had just finished eating when we heard Christmas caroling down the hall. The following year, 1976, I sold my machinery. I bought a slide-in camper for my 1975 GM pickup truck from Lloyd Faust. My wife, daughter, grandson, and Chihuahua dog all headed to Vancouver, BC.

Michael, my grandson, had the best view; he slept on the top bunk by the window. Cindy and Lena would change seats often. I stopped at a Shell station for gas. I paid for the gas and left the station, but we didn't know that the dog had followed me out of the truck. Approximately twenty-five miles later Cindy missed the dog. She called for "Chico" but there was no answer. I was going about sixty-five miles an hour and slowed to stop at another station. I wanted to call the Shell station where I had stopped to get gas. The woman in the station gave me a hard time about using the phone. I told her that I am a truck driver, and I use the phone all the time and would put the charges on my credit card. She finally let me use the phone after some convincing. When I did speak to the man at the Shell station, he saw the dog running around. I told him that I would pay him to keep the dog until we returned. Later, as we approached the station, I saw a light brown spot in the middle of the road. The dog had been run over. When I asked the attendant what had happened, he said he got busy, and the dog got away before he could catch him. We gathered the dog and buried him beside the road. We had a service for him and sang songs from the hymnal book which we always had in the truck. Cindy asked if dogs go to heaven. I told her a story of a little boy who loved his daddy, and when his daddy died, the boy cried and asked why Jesus had taken him away. I said there are also little children in heaven, and Jesus wanted your dad to fix the toys for those children. The lad said, "But I need him here to fix my toys." I said, "Well, my friend, we shall ask Jesus when we get there." Then the little boy said, "Yes, and I shall ask Jesus also about your pet." We had a great trip from Ontario to Vancouver visiting my second oldest sister Sophie and family. We all had a good time. We returned home over the United States and saw the Rocky Mountains. We saw lovely places. Everyone enjoyed the trip, especially my wife, because she didn't have to do any cooking. Michael enjoyed himself with Cindy. Cindy was allowed to stand at a tepee between two Indians while Michael looked on.

At one point of our travel to Vancouver, I stopped for gas and food and asked the man how far it was to a KOA Campground. He said it's miles from here, but said I could use his electricity. We were all glad that we could sleep in our camper. It had all the facilities. As we took off I saw the funnel of a tornado. We took off. I could still see the funnel as we put miles behind us. That was a close call. I'm glad it didn't come in the middle of the night. I'm not sure which province we were in.

Cindy standing between two Indians while Michael looks on.

Cindy and my wife ready to go on the trip to Vancouver.

This picture is of Lake Louise, in Canada.

Here we are in Vancouver; we were on this swinging bridge. It was scary at first; hundreds of feet down below us was a river. The lady on the right is my sister Sophie, behind her is her husband John, and standing in front of her is my grandson Michael. My wife Lena is on the left, and I in the front. We all had a wonderful time.

Shortly after we came home my wife and daughter flew to Germany and Austria to visit my wife's two sisters, two brothers, and their wives. Cindy enjoyed herself, in spite of having a hard time talking German with her cousins. Here at home it was difficult to teach them German when we wanted to learn English. We did learn English from our children as they brought literature home to study; then we always read it in German. We both had a hard time learning to speak English.

**My wife Lena and my daughter Cindy on their trip to Austria.
While there they took a ferry trip.**

My wife's parents in Austria.

My wife's second oldest brother Karl, left center, and his wife, far left, and Karl's father Fredrick Kroh, right center. The young man on the far right is unknown to me.

My wife with her two sisters and brother in Austria.

John Johnson offered me a trucking job. He taught me how to drive a double axle truck with sixteen gears. He was very good and patient with me. My boss was also a Purina Dealer. While I was working for him, their teenage son was killed on the way to a church function. He was a fine young man. The Johnson's also had a daughter; she and my daughter Cindy were friends. Today their daughter is married to a dairy farmer. They also had another son who was a cattle dealer. I drove for John for two years. Every time I came home from driving, my boss's wife, Joanne, would ask me about the ring around my belly. I told her that is because the steering wheel was too big. She just said, "Sure, John, sure."

One day I was sent to my boss's brother to deliver things for them. He was also a dairy farmer. While there I saw such nice little dogs; they were so cute. They asked me if I wanted one. After 3 or 4 weeks I went there again. Then they gave me one; in turn I gave it to my daughter Cindy. She was so thankful, so happy.

Sometime later my boss asked me to pick up a load of feed and then deliver it. While on the highway driving about 60 mph, suddenly I saw that my left front wheel came loose and rolled off in front of the truck and ended up in a ditch. Was I ever scared! I never touched the brakes; I geared the truck down and down to a stop. I got out of my cab. Shocked that my front wheel was gone, I checked all the others, and they were fine. I started walking to bring my wheel back. Meanwhile, a man stopped and allowed me to use his cell phone. I told my boss what had happened, he told me he would send someone out to me. Standing next to the truck, I was surprised that the truck didn't tip over. It probably would have tipped to the front on the left, if it hadn't had such a heavy load (about 20 tons) – what a blessing!

On another occasion, my boss asked me to go to Hamilton to pick up a load of soy meal to deliver to a mill. I'm glad I knew the area. Up to that point where I had to make a left turn into the country road, the road I was on was good driving. As soon as I made that turn, I wanted to give the truck more gas. I felt the rear end of the truck start to fishtail. I knew that it was icy, and ever so dark. I drove up to a big tree on the right and stopped. I knew that from this point, it was downhill, so I decided to wait. A few minutes had passed when a pickup truck came by, and the driver allowed me to use his cell phone. It was about 5 A.M. or 6 A.M. I called my boss and told him it wouldn't be safe to drive downhill; I didn't want to take that chance. He told me to stay there. He would call the mill, and the person there, in turn, would call the township to grade the hill. So he called the mill, and the township was notified. They came out after an hour or two, scraped the ice crisscross, and sanded the hill. I then felt safe to drive down the hill. If I hadn't done this, I could have overturned the truck and spilled all the soy. Also, I could have gotten hurt.

One winter, about a year and a half later, I went to pick up a twenty-ton truckload of corn to take to my boss's brother. We had lots of snow, and I followed the road that the snowplow opened. The truck's rear hind wheels came too close to the end of a culvert and slipped into the ditch, over-turning the truck on its right side. I had no choice but to climb down and stand on the passenger door. I was so ashamed that I had overturned a twenty-ton truck of corn. While I was waiting for someone to come, the devil came to me and said, "You see; what good is it to go to church?" Immediately, I thought about what my sons would say when they came home from Sunday school, which was, "When the devil comes, tell him to 'get thee behind me, Satan.'" Meanwhile, a man drove by the accident scene and walked up to the truck and saw me standing on the passenger door. He asked first, "Are you okay?" I said, "Yes," and he reached down and pulled me out. How grateful I was to him. I made a call to my boss and told him what had happened. The first question he asked me was if I was all right. I told him that I was shook up. He told me he was coming right away and that he would stop to pick up my wife. It took hours to suck the spilled corn into another truck. I am not sure who drove the truck to be repaired. The insurance company advised my boss to let me go, but he said he would not. I was so thankful to him for keeping me on.

About John Johnson: I am so sorry that I overturned your truck with about 20 ton of corn. I wish I could have compensated you with some money, as you know that things cost a lot of money to start and to keep going. Honestly, I lost a lot of money. Otherwise I would have helped you. Once again I'm so sorry. All I can say is I enjoyed working for you. I thank you, John Johnson, for giving me the chance. I really enjoyed trucking. Thank you, John; you're the best man I know.

In the meantime, I had my two farms for sale or lease. One day, when I came from driving the truck, Lena told me that we were going to have company; she would not tell me who. I soon learned that Mike and Lona Karst drove in. I welcomed them. Lena and I were glad that they came to visit. They asked about my farm, but nothing definite had been decided to buy or lease.

On November 22, 1978, my boss John Johnson sent me home with a truck to have a good rest. Later in that afternoon I drove to Hamilton,

Ontario to pick up soy meal for hog farmers. My wife reminded me that she would drive Karl to his ear doctor to check out his operation. My daughter Cindy came home from school, and she asked if she could go along with Mom, so that after the doctor's visit they could go Christmas shopping. How could I take that away from her? I said, "Sure. Enjoy the trip." She turned around and said, "Thanks, Dad."

I worked all night, and on the way home, I stopped at Woodstock at Purina, to pick up things that John had ordered. On the way home, I also stopped at my favorite restaurant. The lady that served me asked if I heard about the accident that took place on Highway 86. I said, "No, I never heard about it. What happened?" I asked. She did not know much about it, only that she heard on the radio the police were waiting for a man to come home in order to go to KW Hospital in Kitchener to identify the bodies. I said to her that I felt sorry for that man already for when he finds that out. Then I asked her about the color of the car, and she said that it was a reddish color. In hindsight, I was glad that I didn't think of my wife's car, as hers was light brown. I finished my cheeseburger and left.

I had to make two large "S" curves. I drove not even knowing that I had made those curves, because my mind was on "the poor man when he finds out about the accident." Little did I know that two hours later the police were waiting for me (I was that "poor man"). All of a sudden, I saw a police officer, along with my neighbor, come in. He had a sour face. The officer asked me if I was Mr. John Hunyady. I said, "Yes." The officer took a big grip on my arm and said that he was so sorry to inform me that my wife Magdalena, age 50, my daughter Cynthia, age 16, my son Karl, age 23, my daughter-in-law Debbie, age 27, and my granddaughter Karin, age 1 year, were all killed on Highway 86 by a five ton truck. I could not help but think of the woman in the restaurant who first told me about this accident. I believe with all my heart that God prepared me by hearing this from her. I am so glad that the Johnson's were not at home that day. If they had been at home, the police would have been able to pick me up in a matter of minutes; the shock would have been more severe. When I heard what the police told me, I was so mad at God. With fists raised, I asked God, "Why? What have they done? What have I done?" Then I turned to God to ask God for His forgiveness for my outburst and ask His help to get through it.

I asked the police if I could make one phone call. The result of the phone call I learned three years later in 1981 when I drove to Florida to the

Christian retreat in Bradenton on vacation. The police took me to pick up my son. My neighbor's wife, as a nurse, sat next to me. We also picked up a minister that my wife and I enjoyed hearing. Shortly before we entered the hospital I met a man by the name of Murray Johnson who I knew for years. I drove trucks for Murray's brother John. Murray was the first man who I told that my dear family had been killed, that they were in the hospital. That was in November, 1978. About one week ago he called me. I cried for happiness to have heard from him. He may come to see me in January, 2011, Lord willing.

As soon as we arrived at the KW Hospital, the coroner came to me and said that my family members didn't suffer at all. The minister went in first to identify the bodies. When he came out, we debated whether my son or I should go in next to see them. The minister suggested that I as the father should be the one to go in to see them. I was shocked to see everyone in plastic bags. My little granddaughter was in a small plastic bag on the windowsill. My son was in the freezer. The funeral arrangement was made by Robert Trench who was the funeral director in Listowel. There were about fifteen hundred people at the funeral. My wife, daughter, and son were buried behind the country church that my wife fell in love with, in the Brotherston Cemetery. Because the church was sold to a Mennonite group, Harold Srigley and I went to ask for permission from the Mennonite group to carry out my wife's wish to be buried there. It was all right with them, but no flowers were allowed. My boss John Johnson called Purina in Woodstock and told them about what happened to my family. They all knew me, and I had just been there to pick up a load only two and a half hours before the accident. Purina sent one of the biggest wreaths I have ever seen, and it said, "To the Hunyady Family. May they rest in peace."

After the funeral, I drove to two or three Mennonite farmers. I just wanted to know where the accident happened. I am sure the reason nobody wanted to tell me was that they thought that if I knew exactly where it was, that I would put up five crosses and flowers. That's the reason nobody told me exactly. That's why I couldn't put anything up.

Following are pictures of the accident, stories, and obituaries courtesy of the Listowel Banner newspaper, Ontario, Canada.

November, 1978
Listowel newspaper article, Ontario, Canada, about the accident.
(Courtesy of the Listowel Banner.)

Family of five killed in highway collision

Five persons, all members of the same family, were killed on Thursday, Nov. 23, when their car skidded on slushy pavement just east of Dorking and crossed Highway 86 into the path of an oncoming delivery truck.

Funeral services for the victims were held at the Robert Trench Funeral Home, Listowel, on Monday at 2 P.M.

Killed in the collision were the driver of the car, Magdalena Hunyady, 50, her son Karl, 23, daughter Cynthia, 16, all of RR 1, Gowanstown; daughter-in-law Debby, Karin, 1, both of RR 3,. Listowel.

Police say the eastbound car skidded on slushy, slippery pavement, crossed the centre line into the path of a Gay Lea Foods delivery truck, driven by David Palmer, 28, of RR 2, Puslinch. The collision occurred about 9:30 A.M. on Highway 86, about two km east of Dorking. It was raining at the time of the accident.

Police say the truck driver swerved onto the right shoulder of the highway in an attempt to avoid the car but was unsuccessful and hit it broadside. Mr. Palmer was not injured in the collision.

There were no charges made in connection with the accident and there will be no inquest. A Kitchener OPP spokesman said that coroner Dr. E.R.S. Wyatt of Elmira was satisfied the accident was a result of slippery roads.

It is believed Magdalena Hunyady was born Jan. 10, 1928, in Yugoslavia to the late Frederick Kroh and his wife, the late Katrina Stieb. After her marriage to John Hunyady, the couple resided in Kitchener before moving to RR 1, Gowanstown in 1963.

She is survived by her husband, John Hunyady Senior, of RR 1, Gowanstown; three sisters, Mrs. George (Sophie) Plein of Elmira, Mrs. Margaret Mauer of Austria and Mrs. Katrina Goettel of Germany; two brothers, Karl Kroh of Austria and one grandson.

Karl Hunyady, 23, was born May 5, 1955, in Kitchener. He worked on the family farm at RR 1, Gowanstown. He is survived by his father and by one brother, John Hunyady Jr. of RR 3, Listowel.

Cynthia Hunyady, 16, was born Nov. 2, 1962, in Kitchener. She was a grade 11 student at Norwell District Secondary School in Palmerston. She is survived by her father and one brother.

Mrs. Deborah Ann Hunyady, 26, of RR 3, Listowel was born Jan. 2, 1952, in Listowel.

She is survived by her husband John F. Hunyady Jr. of RR 3, Listowel; one son Michael, at home; her parents Kenneth and Anna Mae (Holman) Illman; one sister, Teresa Illman of Kitchener; and five brothers, Robert Illman, Walter Illman, Reginald Illman, Wayne Illman Steven Illman, all of Williamsford.

Karin Hunyady, 1 of RR 3, Listowel was born Nov. 25, 1976, in Kitchener to John Hunyady and his wife, the late Deborah Ann (Illman) Hunyady. She is survived by her father; one brother, Michael, at home; maternal grandparents Mr. and Mrs. Ken Illman, and her paternal grandfather John Hunyady Sr.

Rev. James Stanley of Listowel conducted the funeral services on Monday, Mrs. Magdalena Hunyady, her son Karl and daughter Cynthia were buried at Brotherston Cemetery. Mrs. Deborah Ann Hunyady and her daughter Karin were buried at Elma Centre Cemetery, in Atwood.

Listowel newspaper article, Ontario, Canada, November 1978.
(Courtesy of the Listowel Banner.)

KILLED IN LISTOWEL-AREA CRASH
Mourners pay tribute to five dead
By Sheila Hannon, Record Staff Writer

Listowel – Words couldn't describe their sorrow. But actions did.

Mourners overflowed the funeral home here Monday to pay tribute to the five members of the Hunyady family killed Thursday in a highway crash.

Flowers banked the chapel walls, eyes were crying, faces pinched.

Outside, a blustery snowstorm made driving treacherous much the way it did the day the Hunyady car skidded on a snow-covered highway and was struck broadside by a truck.

The driver of the car, Lena Hunyady, 50; her children Karl, 23, and Cindy, 16, her daughter-in-law Deborah, 26, and granddaughter Karin, 1, were killed in the crash on Highway 86 about 12 kilometers west of Elmira.

They were on their way to Kitchener to keep an appointment Karl had with a doctor.

"It's a real shock for families in the area," said Wallace Township Reeve Rae Bender, who lives three miles from John Hunyady Sr., Mrs. Hunyady's husband. "When you see five caskets—young people and a baby—it's kind of shocking."

Both Karl and his sister, Cindy, a Grade 11 student at Norwell secondary school, Palmerston, were living at home on the farm their parents owned northwest of Gowanstown, in 1963, after living in Kitchener since they were married in 1952.

Karin, who lived with her parents Deborah and John Jr. at RR 3, Listowel, would have celebrated her second birthday two days after the fatal car crash.

Deborah, a part-time worker at the Atwood Cheese Factory, is survived by her husband, a son Michael, 10, her parents, Kenneth and Anna Mae Illman of Williamsford, five brothers and one sister.

"It's just heartbreaking," said Yvonne Gedcke, a next-door neighbor to John Sr. "It's hard to describe... It's...heartbreaking." She said, searching for words.

"This is a very close community. We're trying to do as much as we can..."

During the last few days the neighbors pitched in, cleaning, baking and opening their homes to grieving family and friends.

Larry and Elaine Ash's home across the road from the Hunyadys became a central gathering point.

"The neighbors were wonderful—you only had to phone and ask them for anything you wanted," Mrs. Ash said.

About 85 floral tributes flanked the caskets in the Robert Trench funeral home in addition to a number of memorial donations.

More than 1,500 paid their respects at the funeral home and about 450 attended services Monday, said Robert Trench, funeral director.

"It's a touching thing just to see how the neighbors stand by me at this time. I really appreciated that," John Sr. said

"Without these neighbors and friends—and the grace of God, without His help and strength, I wouldn't be able to endure all this and face it."

M dear neighbors and friends. May the Lord bless you all for being there for me.

John Hunyady

(Courtesy of the Listowel Banner.)

HUNYADY—In loving memory of a dear wife, Lena Hunyady, a daughter, Cynthia, a son, Karl, a daughter-in-law, Debby, and a granddaughter, Karin, who died suddenly as the result of a car accident, November 23, 1978.

> Remembrance
> We take for granted
> One another –
> Each and every day.
> The smile you'd wear –
> Telling me you'll be there
> At the close of another day.
> We take for granted
> When we see and hear –
> Of other tragedies;
> That never this,
> Would come our way –
> From this I gained
> My solitude.
> We take for granted
> Time we'll spend,
> Of yet another day
> A day I'll have
> Just you and me –
> Of words I've left
> Locked within the heart of me.
> We plan our lives
> From day to day,
> Yes – even from year to year.
> Forgetting –
> Lives can and will
> Be taken
> On to eternity.
> And now as we think
> Of yesterday –
> That cold November morn'
> We recall the times –
> Of the love we shared
> And of my smiling family

I praise my Lord and Savior,
For the way He carried
And lifted me on through
The sorrow and grief
Reminding me –
You've taken them
"Your faith will see you through"
Ever remembered by husband, father and grandfather, John Hunyady.

(Courtesy of the Listowel Banner.)

HUNYADY—In loving memory of my dear wife, Lena Hunyady, who passed away, November 23, 1978. When I saw you first, you looked very good to me. The longer we were together, I liked you more and more. Do you remember our first trip to Niagara Falls? I'm glad we both learned about it in school. I started to love you each time we were together, and then we got married. You made me the happiest man in the world. As time went by even on the farm we worked very well together. Do you remember when you brought lunch out to me? While I was plowing we took some time for ourselves in the forest. I will love you as long as I live. Some day we will be together again. We will see each other, as we are. We will be together with Jesus the author and finisher of our faith.

Your loving husband forever in my heart, John.

My dear wife Lena.

My dear wife Lena and I coming home from the country church.

(Courtesy of the Listowel Banner.)

HUNYADY—In loving memory of a dear mother and grandmother Magdalena who passed away one year ago, November 23, 1978.

A wonderful mother, woman and aid.

One who as better God never made:

A wonderful worker, so loyal and true.

One in a million – mother was you.

Just in your judgment, always right

Honest and liberal, ever upright;

Loved by your friends, all you knew

A wonderful mother – mother was you

Sadly missed and ever remembered by son John and grandson Michael.

Beloved mother and grandma, Magdalena.

My beloved son, Karl, may you rest in peace.

My beloved son Karl.

(Courtesy of the Listowel Banner.)

HUNYADY—In loving memory of my dear son, Karl Hunyady, who passed away November 23, 1978.

Karl you were a good night worker,

I loved your workmanship.

I love you and miss you, from your Dad, John.

(Courtesy of the Listowel Banner.)

HUNYADY—In loving memory of a dear sister and aunt Cynthia, and a dear brother and Uncle Karl who passed away November 23, 1978.

We often think of days gone by,

When we were all together;

A shadow o'er our lives has cast,

Our loved one's gone forever.

Sadly missed by brother John and nephew Michael.

(Courtesy of the Listowel Banner.)

HUNYADY—In loving memory of my dearest daughter, Cindy Hunyady, who passed away a year ago, November 23, 1978.

Cindy, to my dearest sweetheart,

thinking back to a conversation we

had, you asked me do you know what

you are? I answered, I am your Dad,

she replied, yes, you are my Dad and also a turkey.

I love you and miss you, from your Dad, John.

My beloved daughter Cindy in Austria, 1976.

My two sisters; on the left, Rosie, and on the right, Sophie, from Vancouver, B.C.

(Courtesy of the Listowel Banner.)

HUNYADY—In loving memory of a dear wife and mother Deborah Ann, who passed away one year ago, November 23, 1978.

We are sad within our memory,
Lonely are our hearts today,
For the one we loved so dearly
Has forever been called away.
We think of her in silence:
No eye may see us weep,
But many silent tears are shed
When others are asleep.

Ever remembered and sadly missed by husband John and son Michael.

(Courtesy of the Listowel Banner.)

HUNYADY—Deborah Ann, in loving memory of a dear daughter and sister who passed away one year ago, November 23, 1978.

This month comes back with sad regret,
It brings back a day we will never forget,
God broke our hearts to prove to us
He only takes the best.
The blow was hard, the shock severe
We never knew her time was near.
We miss her more than anyone knows
As each day passes, our emptiness grows.
The tears we shed will wipe away,
The ache in our hearts will always stay.
No one knows the grief we bear,
When the family meets and she's not there,
You left so suddenly, your thought unknown,
But you left us memories we are proud to own.

Sadly missed by Dad, Mom, sister and brothers.

(Courtesy of the Listowel Banner.)

HUNYADY—In loving memory of two very dear friends.Debby and Karin who passed away one year ago, November 23, 1978.

There is nothing as treasured and nothing as rare,
As the love a girl and friend can share.
Through joy and through laughter,
Through sorrow and tears,

A closeness developed
That grew with the years.
This love that we shared
Doesn't need to be spoken,
It's a wonderful bond that can never be broken.
For you who have a close friend,
Treasure her with care,
Because you'll never know the heartache,
When you turn and she's not there.
Always in our hearts, Cheryl, Brian and Phillip.

My son's wife Deborah.

(Courtesy of Listowel Banner.)

HUNYADY—In loving memory of a dear daughter and sister, Karin Annabelle, who passed away one year ago, November 23, 1978.

No stain was on her little heart.
She had not entered there:
And innocence slept sweetly on
The pale white brow so fair.
She was too pure for this cold earth.
Too beautiful to stay,
And so God's holy angel bore
Our Darling one away.
Lovingly remembered and sadly missed by father John and brother Michael.

(Courtesy of the Listowel Banner.)

HUNYADY—In loving memory of a dear granddaughter and niece, Karin Annabelle, who passed away one year ago, November 23, 1978.

Fondly loved and deeply mourned
Heart of our heart we miss you so,
Often, our darling our tears will flow.
Dimming your picture before our eyes.
But never the one in our heart that lies.
The stars seem dim as we whisper low:
"Our own darling granddaughter and niece
we miss you so!"

Sadly missed by Grandpa and Grandma Illman, aunt and uncles.

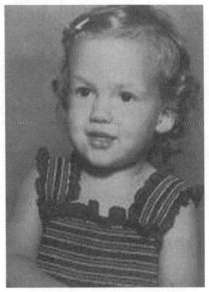

My son Johnny's daughter Karin.

My son's daughter Karin, my beloved granddaughter.

On the left is Mr. Illman; one of his sons is standing in front of him, then Michael, my grandson, my son Johnny, my sister-in-law Sophie from Elmira, my sister Rose, and I.

Mr. and Mrs. Ken Illman and their beloved granddaughter Karin.

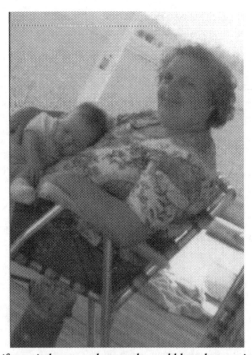

My beloved wife was in heaven as long as she could have her precious grandbaby.

After the funeral, I do not recall exactly who it was, but some-one drove me to my son's house. I was so sorry to see my daughter-in-law's family, the Illmans. Under these circumstances, it was very difficult to see all the aunts and uncles who were dairy farmers. My dear wife and I were very proud to have had our dear daughter-in-law Debbie in our family and Michael, her son from a previous marriage. I found out that these two were inseparable. We always liked that family and knew that Debbie came from a good family and was a good worker. When they moved to the farm, her job was to feed calves and clean their pens. She also made profiles of the calves for the registration under my prefix, "Lone Creek Farms." After the meal, the Illman family went in a room. They formed a circle, joined hands and began to rock slowly, singing, "Bind us together, bind us in love." Every time I hear this song in a church, I can't help but think of the Illmans.

Debbie's father, Kent Illman, wished for Debbie and our granddaughter to be buried in the Illmans' plot. I told them I had no problem with that. They dug somewhat deeper so they could put the baby's coffin on top of her mother. Later, I was taken to my daughter's girlfriend's parents. This man was one of the speakers at the funeral. I had previously met Alex and his wife at our full gospel meetings, and knew them for some time. They took care of me. Someone was always with me 24 hours a day. I walked around like a zombie. After a week or so, John Johns, my lawyer, called and told me to come in and see him in a day. On the way home from my friend's place to the farm, I contracted a thumping headache. I stopped in to see my doctor, and he told me that the only way he could help me was through hypnosis. I told the doctor that I did not believe in hypnotism. I'm not sure how my driving was. I kept thinking how my wife had lost control of her car on a snow-covered icy road; she drove on the other side of the road toward the ditch where a five ton truck hit her broadside. It was not the driver's fault, police told me. I knew the company, not the driver. I drove home and for the first time I sat on my wife's bedside. I took her German Bible and let it fall open at random. It opened on II Thessalonians, 2nd chapter, 3rd verse, where it reads, "Let no man deceive you by any means." The way that I read it was that the doctor wanted to deceive me. I said, "Thank you, Jesus, for that word." I then fell asleep and slept like a baby. My headache was gone, and I have not had a headache since.

Knowing that my wife was going to drive to the doctor and shopping, I drove her car to the mechanic that I knew for years. I asked him to check out the car from top to bottom, which included the oil change and whatever else the car needed. Two weeks after the accident, I went back to the mechanic. I asked him if he was sure that the car was in good shape, and he said, "For the last time, John, I am going to tell you that there was nothing wrong with your wife's car." I was satisfied.

I never had a chance to see my daughter graduate from high school or go to a prom or to a daughter and dad dance. With tears in my eyes, I have thought how much we would have enjoyed it.

A while after the funeral I came in contact with my wife's niece in Ottawa, Canada. I reminded her that since her Aunt Lena was no longer alive, she didn't have to call me "Uncle John." She said right away that as long as she lives she will call me "Uncle John." I told her that makes me very happy.

Two or three months later, I felt comfortable to drive my pickup truck. I went to the Purina office and everyone wanted to know how it happened. I thanked them personally for their cards, prayers and the nicest wreath. At the funeral home, I had seen that Mike and Lona were there. They told me that they were so glad that they saw Lena again. We hugged, kissed and cried together. I believe with all my heart that God arranged that we meet again. I am so glad that the Karsts were obedient to the still small voice. I wondered if anyone could imagine if they hadn't come. They would have felt awful; he passed on a few years later. I was also very grateful for my brother-in-law George, who has passed on, and his wife Sophie Plein. They called family and friends to notify them of the accidental death of my family.

My brother-in-law George and I.

At the funeral, I touched every casket. I told them I would see them again and that I loved them.

Whenever I was alone, I cried out to God and asked Him, "What am I going to do?" I had a nice family, and I had looked forward to seeing them grow into mature people and watching them have a family of their own. I had told my daughter that I would be the happiest father in the whole wide world to lead her to the front of the altar and give her away in marriage. I know that they are with Jesus, the author and finisher of their faith. I read in the Bible that love and forgiveness releases us from Satan's hold and from the attachment of reliving the pain of memory again and again. Then I called the driver that hit my family's car. I assured him that I had called in peace, and I just wanted him to know that I am calling in the name of Jesus and that I forgive him for driving into my family. I heard a big sigh and a thank you. I was also a truck driver and knew how he felt. After my family's accident, the doctor ordered me not to drive a commercial truck or work for a while due to the shock of the accident.

During the winter of 1978, after the accident, I was invited to spend Christmas with my sister Sophie and her husband John Bidner in Vancouver, BC. I went to see the polar bear swimmers coming out of a door in their bathing suits and jumping into icy water. I walked a lot in that city. My sister gave me the number of a bus that would take me home. One day I went to a massage studio; a lady massaged me; I had my underwear on. While she worked on me she told me that she had a son who was killed in a motorcycle accident. She was (furious) angry that she was left alone. I asked her what she was going to do about it; she said she was going to buy and take some pills that would kill her. When I asked her, "What would you do if you had three members of your family killed?" she said, "Oh, I would have killed myself long ago." By then I was dressed, and I said to her, "Ma'am, I'm standing in front of you telling you that I lost five members of my family." When she heard that, she said that she was going home to flush all her pills down the drain. She also told me that from that day on she would not complain any more; she would start going to church. She could see that my faith in the good Lord helped me.

In 1979, I was invited to spend Easter with my oldest sister and her family in Germany. I went to visit my brother's wife and daughter Sabine in Nuremberg, Germany. My brother had passed away of cancer about twenty years before. While visiting them, Sabine's mother asked her if she would show Uncle John the city. We started walking and I said to her, "Since I am here, I would like to brush up on my German." Sabine said, "Uncle John, I am going to school to learn English as I would like to learn how to speak English. It's one thing to learn English, but it's another thing to learn how to speak it." I had a Euro pass which allowed me to travel all over Europe. I went to Norway to a full gospel convention. When I came back, I asked my brother-in-law John Zautner, if someone would be willing to go with me at my expense to the village where I was born. He asked, "How do you remember the house and the mill?" I said, "Very well." He said that I should live with those memories and not go back. As badly as I wanted to go, I took his advice and did not go. I didn't want to travel alone. I am very grateful, and cherish the memories and pictures that I do have. I didn't feel up to undertaking the trip by myself.

I remember reading about people from my village who worked hard to make enough money so they could take a vacation to the village where they were born and grew up in. They saw that the herdsmen who minded the cattle of the village never lived in a house. At that point of time they saw that these herdsmen were in the forest and would drag a tree to their homes. They would break through the door and drag the tree inside and put it in the fireplace. As it burned, they would then move the tree up so that it was always in the fire. They never knew to cut the tree down and then cut it up and burn it a piece at a time, and not the whole tree!

After that, I went to Austria to visit my wife's family. When I was there, my sister-in-law took me to her church and said that I should give my testimony of how the Lord has helped me through my tragedy. I said that I believed with all my heart that the Lord Jesus was with me right from the beginning.

Karl was the next member of my wife's family I visited. I had never met him before. My wife told me that if I ever needed to go to Austria, to go to Karl. When I arrived, he greeted me with open arms, and we spent some time together. After awhile, I asked him about his brother Fritz. He is the oldest brother of my wife. He told me that he was in the hospital sick with stomach problems. I asked if we could go and visit him, and he said we could on Sunday. He also said that his daughter had built a house and tomorrow they were going to pour cement for the sidewalk around the house. Early Sunday morning there was a knock on the door; a messenger from the hospital came to inform us that Fritz had passed away. Karl felt so bad. At the funeral, I met all of my wife's family except my father and mother-in-law. At the funeral was the first time I had ever seen a German military burial. They had six German soldiers saluting with rifles and shooting in the air.

I then took a train from Paris to Berlin, Germany. I started to see high fences. I stood near a window. The further we went, the queasier I became. At one point the train stopped and I saw two people in light brown uniforms board the train. The lady came to me and asked for the train fare. I showed her that we are in Germany. This lady told me that we are not in Germany, but that we are in the DDR. I thought to myself, "Be careful, don't say too much." She asked for my passport, but I only had my Euro pass. There was a silence for a moment. The man that she came in with asked if everything was OK. She asked me to pay the fare from Paris to the DDR, $80.00. She thanked me for the $80.00. I'm sure it was mostly because I didn't have all my papers. She could have arrested me knowing the situation. On her way out, I said to her thank you in German.

I was at the Berlin Wall in Germany in 1979.

My brother's wife and his daughter Sabine.   My brother Michael (kneeling) at work. He was also a flour miller in Germany.

My wife's oldest brother Fritz and his family in Austria.

I visited the Berlin Wall. There was a platform erected for people to sit on to see the other side (East Zone). While sitting there it happened that a rabbit hopped around the mines. Everybody shooed the rabbit away. The platform was only about 25–30 feet away from the wall. All around the mines was a small picket fence. There was a busload of people who wanted to go to the East; it took a while because we all had to go through customs at the border. Once on the other side, the farther the bus ride, the more nervous I became. In every window there was a red flag. Later, I was glad to be back on the West side.

I went to Holland to see the beautiful tulips. There I saw a windmill for the first time. They have four sections to catch the wind. The difference between their mills and ours was that the building and millstones were much smaller. Ours were driven by water and theirs by wind.

Upon arriving home from Germany, Mike called me. He asked me if I would drive their trailer full of corn and I agreed. I drove to the scale, and then unloaded. I loved the job. When I returned, the other trailer was waiting for me. Mike was able to keep on combining because he had a 3-4 ton holding tank. It worked out all right. One day, Mike told me that the next day we were going to my place to harvest the corn. Lona called and asked where I was; I told her that I was at my place. She asked me to wait as she would bring me my food basket. While waiting for my lunch basket, in my mind, I saw my own herd of Holstein cows grazing or eating chopped up corn from the wagon that I had brought down from the silo. I saw my children playing. I saw my dear wife throwing me kisses. I saw her in the same nightgown from the moments that we shared just a few hours before her passing. The reason for those kisses from my wife was because she knew that I had to drive all night. There is where I saw her the last time alive.

Lona Karst came and brought me the food basket. I told her that I just could not come back here. That it was too hard for me. Lona saw me crying. Mike called me to drive their trailer once he started on a different farm.

After one and a half years being a widower, I met and dated a fine lady in Kitchener. She was a director of some kind of business. We dated for about a year and a half. By then she found out that because of the shock I went through from the accident, I was not the man I used to be. After a few more dates, I told her that we should not see each other any more.

One day, I was at a police station to bail out a young man. I had known his mother; we used to live in the same complex. I accidentally bumped into another young man who turned out to be the son of the lady who I was dating. The first question that came from this young man was, "What have you done to my mom?" I asked, "What have I done?" He then told me that his mom had begun to attend church and that she sang in the choir. I asked if she was happy, and he said she was. I then turned to him and said, "Oh that's wonderful; something good did come out of our relationship."

Later in 1981, I went to Florida on a vacation to a Christian retreat for about two or three months. There I met men who also belonged to the full gospel chapters. Some came from several different states and Canada. They remembered praying for someone who had lost five members of his family in Canada. The men wanted to know what had happened. Although I did tell some of the men the horrible details of the accident, I was too distraught to continue to repeat it every time someone asked.

During the retreat I met a lovely lady from New Jersey whose name was Emma. We went to services and ate meals together. She had a room at the retreat while I slept in my camper. We decided one day to drive to Cypress Gardens in Winter Haven, Florida, but along the way stopped at the Frostproof Assembly of God Church. Emma asked, "Have you ever been in an African American Church?" I told her, "No, I have never attended one." The congregation was predominately African American. I had never been in a church like that. It was different from what I was familiar with. I saw an elderly lady who was playing the drums. I was amazed at how she was really in control of them while she was playing. She really looked like she enjoyed herself. The songs were different, and the preaching was right on. We had a good time and walked away from the church blessed. Everyone was so friendly to us and treated us like family; they asked if we would take pictures with their children. My lady friend had all white hair.

We then continued on our journey and finally made it to Cypress Gardens. We enjoyed the water skiing shows and had a fun day together. Emma told me that she was a divorced woman and had one divorced son. She had a daughter named Pat, who was married to a fine man. They had tried for years for her to become pregnant, and up to that day, they were unsuccessful. The more we spent time together, the more I began to like Emma. After two weeks at the retreat, she had to fly back home. I drove her to the airport. She said if you want to know where I live, bring two bags of oranges and one grapefruit. When I drove back home to Canada after I left the retreat, I stopped to see her. I visited her for two or three days and slept in my camper while I was there.

On that Sunday, we attended a full gospel church of the kind familiar to me. We sang "Turn Your Eyes Upon Jesus" and many other songs that

I knew. In time Emma came to visit me. By this time our relationship began to develop into something more serious. Within three quarters of a year later, we were married in Ontario close to Kitchener. Before we were married, we had an understanding that both she and her mother would come to live with me in Kitchener. I told her that my heart and soul were there, and I did not want to live anywhere else. We found a beautiful two bedroom apartment on the 16th floor. At the wedding, my sister Maria, her husband and their son Michael were there on vacation from Germany. They took part in our wedding. While we were waiting for the visas for Emma and her mom, we stayed in her house in New Jersey. In order for me to apply for a green card, I had to stand in front of a judge raising my right hand and tell the judge that I would not be a burden to New Jersey and that I had my own money. I wonder why the other states do not adopt these ideas.

Emma's son on the left; Emma, my wife, and I, in 1982 on our Wedding Day in Kitchener, Canada. Standing in front of me is Michael, my grandson. Standing behind him is my son John. To the right of John are Emma's daughter and her husband John.

**My wife Emma and I bought this trailer. This little girl came to visit
from the campgrounds where we stayed.**

I was also offered a trucking job by an African American lady. She said
that I should give her business card to the Supervisor of the plant. In turn,
he gave me a trucking job working for Cumberland Farms Dairy delivering
products to their stores. I delivered to South Jersey and Delaware hoping the
visas would come soon. I delivered bread, donuts, and the Cumberland Farm
Dairy products. I was at the same stores every other day. Throughout the years
some drivers wanted to go on vacation. My boss asked me to drive with some
of the other drivers to get to know the routes. Approximately three years later
I had been in every store. One day my boss told me to deliver a trailer full of
ice to every Cumberland Farms Dairy Store. One time, I came to a store and
the lady had three large freezers. After I filled them all up, naturally there was a
lot of water on her floor. She asked me to clean up all that water. I told her that
was her job. She said, "I was a sergeant in the U.S. Army." I asked her to sign
my delivery; if not, I would sign it. She knew if she didn't sign it, her supervisor
would have a good talk with her. I had many occasions like this.

One day my supervisor told me he wanted me to take a trailer and
go to West Virginia in the morning. I started out early and I had all the
information on my seat. By the time I got there I had spent $25 in tolls
and I had left home with $30. I walked to a bank to ask for money on my
Canadian Credit Card, and the teller told me that it was a drive-in bank.
I told her that I am here with an 18-wheeler, and then she said to come in
with a taxi. I should have asked for her supervisor, but I walked back to

the warehouse. I talked to a lady in the head office on the phone. She said she could help me out, but I had to wait until 10:00 P.M. While I was talking on the phone, the night supervisor overheard me and my dilemma; this kind man lent me $50. I told him that I hadn't eaten all day and that I would mail him the money when I returned home. I accepted his offer and had a hot meal before retiring for the night. When I got home, my wife sent him a check for $50 along with a big thank you note.

While I was living in New Jersey and driving a truck, a new driver was hired, and I was to train him to deliver ice cream to our stores. Some years later, in 1985, I began to work for the same company in Florida doing the same thing. I soon found out that the very same man that I had trained in New Jersey was there. He invited me to come to his parents' house for a Christmas dinner. Everything was great until his sister came with two or three children. They ran right to the Christmas tree. My thoughts wandered back to my own children while they were that age and we celebrated Christmas together. They received no toys, but all the necessary things they needed like clothes. The more I thought about my children, I could not stay in the house any longer and had to get up and excuse myself. I then went outside, sat in my pickup truck, and cried because I was so sorry that I had not been able to afford any more gifts for my children. As years went by, I made more money and was able to afford more gifts for the children; the gifts my boys got were clothes. The truth of the matter was that I did the best I could do at the time for my children, under the circumstances. I didn't know much English.

One day three years later, I came home from work to find the visas had finally arrived. Also, my wife informed me that her daughter Pat was pregnant. All I could say was, "That's great." I asked Emma, "When are we moving to Ontario?" Then she said she did not want to go. I told her that it would be seven or eight months before the baby would be born. In the meantime, Emma's ex-mother-in-law got sick. She was hospitalized, and the doctor told Emma's ex-husband that his mother could no longer live by herself anymore. She would have to live in an old age home. Pat asked her mom if she would mind looking after her grandmother. My wife told Pat that she would have to ask me first. When I came home, my wife asked me if she could. Since I also knew Pat's grandmother, we picked her up and brought her to church with us. I wanted to do something for her. I told my wife that she could look after her under one condition. The condition was that I did not want my wife's ex-husband to come visit his mother except when I was home. My wife said all right.

I was a truck driver, and I really enjoyed my job driving an eighteen wheeler, but I never came home on time. A few times I came home from work somewhat later than usual; Emma's ex-husband was there visiting his mother. I am not sure if my wife ever told him, or she did tell him and he ignored her request. I think she did not take my request seriously. That brought friction between us. I stopped taking showers with her and our intimacy that we once shared became less and less. I do not think for one moment that it took three years for the visas to come. I think they came earlier, and Emma did not want to tell me. She was hoping that Pat would get pregnant and that is exactly what happened. I could not stand the betrayal. I know that if my wife had talked to me, explaining that she was very happy to be a grandma, I also would have feelings and value being a grandpa. Then we could come to an understanding. She said that she would not move with me. I tried to be reasonable with her. After the baby was born, I was really happy for her. I also enjoyed the baby; when she was able to walk, we took her with us to Ontario. We went into a store where they sold all kinds of music. I bought a chicken dance tape; the little girl really enjoyed it. Anytime she was with Grandpa she wanted to hear the chicken dance; when she did hear it she was all smiles. She was slow in talking, so whenever she wanted to hear the tape all she did was raise her shoulders up and down. She really enjoyed it when we danced. She brought much joy into my life.

I had many fine memories of Emma. One of them was when we went to a Hungarian restaurant. There was a Hungarian man making music with his violin. When he approached my table, I asked him if he knew of a certain song. I was surprised I had remembered it. Once he began playing, I started to sing in Hungarian and it was well received by everyone. The song I sang I cannot interpret. While living with her, Emma had many African American friends. One day a call came in that a lady she knew had passed on. When we went to her funeral there were many people. I did not see one tear rolling down their cheeks. They were praising the Lord that she went home to be with Jesus. They sang songs such as "One Day at a Time" and "Sweet Jesus." It seemed like everyone in the church knew the words to those songs. I have never been so encouraged to want to go on with Jesus. There is a brighter day for us as believers in the Lord Jesus Christ. Even before this event I worked and associated with African American people. I have no problems going into their homes because we are all one in Jesus. Years later, there was an African American man who lived in one of my apartments, and I hired him to do all my maintenance work for some of his rent.

While I lived in New Jersey I received a letter from my sister Rose in Ontario informing me that a couple named Low lived in Philadelphia. I remembered them so well; their job in our village was to pull the rope to ring the church bells. I used to help them. Their son Michael, a good friend, had died years before. On one of my visits to the Low's, their daughter and her family came to visit her parents. Was I ever glad that we met again! It had been fifty years since we had seen each other.

**Daughter of the Low's family. We grew up in the same village.
We met again fifty years later.**

In November 1984, I packed up my belongings in my trailer. I had such good memories of all of the times we spent traveling, visiting different states, seeing beautiful mountains and farmlands. I left her, drove to Kitchener, Ontario, and had my Christmas with my son Johnny, Pat, my grandson Michael, and my sister Rose.

I drove down to the west coast of Florida for a vacation at the Christian Retreat in Bradenton. Afterwards, I decided to drive over to the east coast where the sister company to Cumberland Farms was located in Riviera Beach. I inquired about a trucking job. I had worked for that company previously and had all my credentials from the Cumberland Dairy in New Jersey. I spoke with the manager of the dairy who offered me a job to start the following day. I told him that I couldn't. Therefore, he said to start work on June 15, 1985. The manager was very good to me; my first trip was to Miami with the 18-wheeler. I asked how I should orient myself. He said, "If the ocean is on your right then you're facing north." I thought that was easy until I turned myself around a few times, then it was hard. Most of the Cumberland Stores were open 24 hours a day. This helped me with the deliveries. I left early at 7 A.M. and came home at about 2 A.M. – 3 A.M. As time went by I knew the routes and where to go.

Christmas of 1984. I was with my son Johnny, and Pat, my grandson Michael, and my sister, Rose.

My sister Rose, with her friend George, dancing the chicken dance. I loved to see my sister dancing and having fun.

Here is my sister Rose, and her daughter Rosemary, lovely people.
I do miss my sister; anytime I needed information about something in
Europe she would know.

Emma called me and told me there was a marriage seminar at the Praise The Lord Ministry in South Carolina that offered counseling. She had her own room, and I slept in my trailer. The sessions were informative. The last day came, and we all had to make up our minds which way we would go with our marriage. Everyone shared his or her solution. Emma took my hands and said, "John, I want to make things right." I will go home and tell my ex-husband to take his mother home with him, so I can have a life with you. I reached over to her and we kissed each other. I said, "That's great." After one or two days, I drove her to the Charlotte, North Carolina airport. On the way there, she said, "I want to take care of my mother-in-law as long as she lives." I told her that I wanted a divorce. Looking back I can now understand why my wife lied to me. She wanted her own family so badly. If my wife had talked to me, she would have known that I was a reasonable man in any situation and that I understood the importance of family. She said that she did not want to move. Well, I believe I did what I had to do.

Cumberland Farms, where I worked.

My new boss in Florida.

Me at work.

I also met a young boy at the Christian retreat in Florida. His family was from Saskatchewan, Canada. He began to tell me what happened to his family on the airplane. His mother sat next to his grandmother. As they took off, the grandmother, who had never flown before, said, "We really must climb a big hill." Her daughter just said, "Yes, Mom." As they landed in Florida, the daughter showed her mom the airplane they just came off and said, "We came with this thing," and she pointed to the airplane. The grandmother said that the man who drove it must have really known his way.

One day I was at the pool for a swim when I noticed a man with a big robe on and a mug of coffee. In time I met his wife Norma. We would meet in the church hall, at the cafeteria, or at shuffleboard. From that time forward, we saw each other often. Jim, her husband, and I had two things in common—we loved the Lord and we were both truck drivers. He drove for the union, but not me. I slept in my camper. The following year they came with a big recreational vehicle, and they invited me to sleep in their R.V. We had a good time. As time went by they bought a house at Praise The Lord Ministry, in South Carolina. I wanted to drive up to Praise The Lord Ministry area, and I called them to see if they would be home. They told me they had already made other plans for that time period, but they offered their house for me to stay in as long as I wanted. They said they would leave the keys with their neighbor. I had my meals at Praise The Lord Ministry and had a blessed time; I was in their house for one to two weeks. I really felt honored that anyone would offer me, a total stranger, their house. As years went by Norma wrote me some very sad news that her husband had gone to be with the Lord. I wrote her back and gave her my condolences and told her how much I had appreciated our friendship over the years. I am still in contact with Jim's wife.

Jim and Norma Wickman.

One day, I met a lady in the church here in West Palm Beach, Florida. We agreed to go for a swim in the ocean, but she did not feel like getting wet that day. I considered myself a good swimmer, but the under current took me in and I felt helpless. My feet went every which way. I tried to get out of the current, but I could not. At that particular time, I did not know what to do when something like that happened. I started to cry out to the Lord. I prayed, "Lord, please help me; You don't want me to die here." He answered my prayer, because a big wave of water pushed me right to the shore. I was so exhausted once I arrived on the shore; it felt like I was out there for longer than a few moments. My friend helped me get up and to a chair. I said, "This has never happened to me before." Since then, I never have gone into the ocean by myself. All I can say is "Thank you, Jesus, for saving my life again."

Speaking of the ocean, Stan, his grandchildren, and I went once to the ocean, and we really enjoyed that. A big wave came and knocked me over. The children called me back, and then another wave came and knocked me over again. I said, "No more! That is it!" We had a big laugh about that. We enjoyed our conversation that afternoon.

My friend Stan and his grandchildren, from Atlanta, Georgia.
He also helped me with my story.

In 1990, I met a beautiful German lady named Lee. About a year and a half prior to us meeting, her husband had died of cancer. They came over to the United States from Germany to New York. She did not know how to speak the English language, but worked everywhere she could find a job. She also attended night school to learn the language. Some years later, they moved to Florida and she was able to get a job at the Boca Raton Community Hospital. She worked herself up to become the paymaster at the hospital and retired after twenty-five years of service. Today she works as a volunteer at Hospice by the Sea doing the same job of payroll.

My friend Lee and I. She also helped me with my story.

In October of 1991, when Boca Raton Community Hospital had a reward banquet for their employees and honored those who had long-term service with the hospital, Lee invited me to be her escort to the country club. Her boyfriend was traveling that week and was too far away to escort her. The day of the banquet, we had a warning about a hurricane, but we still met at her work location's parking lot. The car that she drove was a big car and helped us to get through the stormy times with strong winds and to pass over the tree limbs on the road. At one point, she said, "Close your eyes." When we arrived, there were many people there, some of whom I knew. Someone approached her and asked if she could be interviewed. There was good food, lots of dancing and entertainment, and all had fun.

In 1993, I had to drive to Miami to become a United States citizen. Lee offered her time to go with me. She did not want me to drive alone. She wanted to keep me company. While driving, she was in contact with her office by cell phone. I am so glad that she came with me for the ride, because I really enjoyed her company.

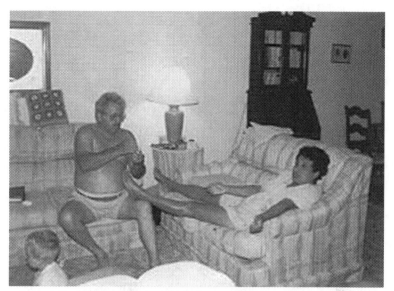

**I am giving Eddie a pedicure, which she enjoyed. We were baby-sitting her
daughter's little boy, from Talladega. He wanted to be with his Grandma.**

In 1994, Lee married her second husband and they invited my lady
friend Eddie and me to their wedding. Everything was so beautiful, and I
knew several other people who attended. When dinner was over and the
table cleared, the dancing began. The musician played one of the most
beautiful Vienna waltzes. This lovely bride came over the dance floor to
me, bowed and asked if she could have the honor to dance with me. I did
the same bow and said, "It would be an honor." As we danced together,
I got very emotional. I started to cry and she said, "Don't you cry on me
now." I promised her that I would not. I always enjoyed her and her new
husband's company.

Where I was working, a group of Creole people who my supervisor and
I worked with invited us to a barbecue. The food was good and tasty. After
that time, they never invited me to return, only my supervisor. Then, after
a while, an order came to my supervisor that he had to lay off one man.
Instead of laying off the Creole man, he laid me off. He kept the Creole
people. I could have gone to the manager to complain, but I did not. The
supervisor should have kept me on because of my seniority. I knew at that
moment that if I went to the manager, he would have told the supervisor
to keep me. I did not want to provoke any anger in the situation, because
I go out of my way to live a peaceful life with everyone.

Bob and Belinda, Eddie, and I, at Lee's wedding.

I was honored to have been invited to Lee and her husband's wedding.

I sold my fifth wheel trailer and my pickup truck in 1995. With the money I received, I purchased two duplex houses that had two bedrooms and one bath. I was financially secure at that time. One of my tenants invited me to a Creole wedding. At the wedding, if I knew a song, I would sing it in German, and they would sing in their language.

My brother-in-law George took this picture of his wife Sophie standing in the doorway, and me at the trailer. They came for a visit from Elmira, Ontario, Canada.

Here I am ready to go to church, standing in front of one of my duplexes.

In 1995, I am standing between my two duplexes.

My son John came from Canada to build me a patio.

Johnny rinsing off his lady friend.

One of my tenants and her children.

I had two friends who would travel every other year from Toronto to Germany to see their families. The ladies were in one room. There was a teenage girl who said that her aunt Gretel's husband had passed on. This lady from Toronto, a mutual friend of Gretel and me, wrote my name and address on a sheet of paper and she said to the girl, "Give this to your aunt." One day, I received a letter from Gretel, I was really surprised. Her first question was, "What have you done with yourself in the last forty years?" I wrote her back, telling her that it would take another forty years to explain what I had done. We corresponded often. My sister Rose in Ontario was so happy that I had heard from Gretel. She invited Gretel and me to come to Canada to her grandson Jeffrey's confirmation. We accepted the invitation. She came to my place, and I gave her my second bedroom. We were so glad to see each other again. I drove her around Florida, and then slowly we drove north, which we both enjoyed. Each of us had a motel room. The further north we drove, the more we enjoyed our trip, especially the changing of the leaves. We drove over mountains, through tunnels, and we rested here and there. Gretel slept with my sister in her house and had a good time at the confirmation.

I am so glad Gretel and I could take part in Jeffrey's confirmation.

Gretel flew back from Toronto; she wrote me that she went often to doctors. Her oldest son wrote me to inform me that his mom had passed on.

I wrote him a letter stating that his mom was a very nice lady, and for him to know that we had a platonic relationship, and may she rest in peace.

My sister Rose on the right, and our friend Gretel, on the left; we hadn't seen her since 1950.

To the right is Andy Gellner's mother, with her grandson Christopher at his confirmation.
To the left is his Grandma Rose Poschner.

139

Rose, my sister, and her lady friend came to visit me; I had a two bedroom apartment. My sister told me that George Romer, who has a condominium, lives in Boynton Beach, Florida. One day we went to visit him, and he told me because he couldn't see too well anymore, he wanted to sell the one bedroom condominium. I thought about my situation, having a two bedroom and no one comes to visit. My sister and lady friends did a lot of work like cleaning, cooking, and looking after the flower garden. About one week before they arrived for a visit, there was a shark attack with a boy on his surf board. The boy was okay; he said that as soon as he felt good again, he would be going back out in the ocean. One day I drove them to Singer Island, which is a beautiful beach and we had a good time and really enjoyed ourselves. We went there a few times, and then it was time for them to leave for home. On their last day, I showed them the clippings of the shark attack in the newspaper I had cut out. My sister said she was glad that I didn't show her the article before we went to the beach. I didn't want to spoil their vacation or the good times we were having.

My sister Rose on the left, and her lady friend on the right.

My sister Rose in front of her friend, watering plants.

Soon after I moved into my condominium, I leased out my apartment for $750 a month. When the first month came for collecting the rent, the lady told me that she could not pay because her husband left her. I soon found out that was only an excuse, because at one point my neighbor called and told me that the lady's husband came home to her at about 7 P.M. or 8 P.M. He then left early in the morning at about 6 A.M. or 7 A.M. She said she was trying to get the money from her husband. I was unsuccessful in getting the money from her. Anytime I got the police involved it cost me money. It took me four months to get her out. Finally a neighbor called me at 1 A.M. or 2 A.M., and told me that she had the moving truck there. I called the sheriff to meet me there. Before I left to go, I told him she had given me a bum check. He said, "Because she gave you a bum check she belongs in jail." The sheriff asked, "What should I do with her?" I said, "Set her free."

While I lived in my second floor condominium, two ladies and a young girl came to visit me, and the little girl was seven or eight years old. She said, "Mr. Hunyady, can I talk to you?" She said, "Sir, you are not getting younger, why did you buy the condominium upstairs?" One day I met Sandy and as months went by, I asked her to move in with me. I am glad that she was with me when I had my heart attack at 2 o'clock in the morning. She called the doctor and the nurse immediately returned the call. She said that I should go directly to JFK Hospital; they will be waiting for me. Sandy drove me there and was with me until 5:00 A.M. She had to go home to get some rest so she could go to work. I let her drive my new Buick car as long as she was living with me.

In February of 1998, I had a six-bypass heart operation. That same month, I lost close to $4,000 in rentals and wages. Two of my apartments were empty. My finances were down, and I could not recoup my losses. I had no choice but to sell my properties at a big loss. I had put thousands of dollars, as well as my heart and soul into those rentals, and I was planning for more. I was out of work for many months because of the heart operation. In 1995 I was the happiest man in the world to know that I have two duplexes and one house with three bedrooms. I was planning for more once I had my 6 bypasses, but I couldn't keep up with my payments. I had to sell the properties for a big loss. I did not know what else to do.

While I was in rehabilitation, two young men wheeled me in for therapy. They put a five pound sandbag on top of my foot, and then asked me to lift it. I asked how high I should lift it; I did very well. Then they tried ten pounds; again I lifted it all the way up. Finally, they tried fifteen pounds; again I lifted my feet all the way up. This all happened the same day. Then they said that I did not need therapy. When I got home I walked around like a mummy. A nurse would come by every other day. Soon she removed some bandages. I could move around. Sandy looked after me. My son John and Pat came from Canada for a visit. After a day they drove to Key West; they enjoyed themselves. When they returned they were with me for a few days. Sandy cooked a delightful meal for us all. She just loves to cook! When I got better she moved out. In time she found herself a man, and after a while, she got married. She invited me to her wedding in Tallahassee, Florida. I met all of her family at her wedding; everybody wanted to know if I was John.

Sandy and I; we enjoyed each other's company.

Here is Sandy on her wedding day, God bless them.

My son Johnny and Pat.

The company that I worked for delivering produce in Okeechobee City, Florida, and surrounding areas would not rehire me because it would be too hard for me physically. I decided to retire for good. While I was recovering from my operation, I was on my crutches walking up and down the steps of the condominium. I could not help but think of the previous conversation I had with the little girl concerning my living in the second floor condominium instead of a first floor condominium. In time, I had all my bandages off and it felt good.

I was at a German function and there were many people having good food and great entertainment. We all had to bring our plates to a place to be washed. We all had some gravy on our plates including another German man, and we looked at one another, and I said, "During the war I would have licked the plate nice and clean." Several other German men around me agreed.

I spent Christmas of 1999 with my family; my son Johnny, Pat, grandson Michael, and my sister Rose. Then I came in contact with the Walkers and told them that I was at my sister's place. I asked them if I could come and visit. Linda, his wife, told me that Bill was coming through Kitchener. Linda made the arrangements for Bill to pick me up at a certain place. My sister Rose drove me there, and Bill picked me up and drove me home to his place.

Bill and Linda have two lovely girls and one young son. Today their son is in Germany in the seminary studying theology to become a German Lutheran Minister. Their children have asked me about the war, and I told them I have never seen such devastation in my life. I said that I got to Germany in 1946 and lived there until my immigration to Canada in 1950. I had a good time there. I like it when people ask questions about my past. I really appreciate the Walkers' daughter Brittany. After being home for two days from my vacation in Kitchener, I was in the hospital with pneumonia. I received a letter from Brittany that she would like to interview me with 24 different questions. She wanted to know if I had noticed any change in people's appearance, lifestyle, clothing, or the way they treat others these day from the way they were when I was growing up. My answer to these questions was, "I grew up in a poor family, and I didn't have much clothing or money. Money changes everything." Brittany started typing. Time went by and I noticed the work became too much for Brittany because she was so involved with other things. Then I asked her to send me all the material she had from starting work on my story.

The Walker family, one of the finest families I know. May the good Lord bless and keep you. Brittany and her husband on their Wedding Day.

In the meantime, I got to know a young man by the name of Garth. He was in the real estate business, and he wanted me to be the manager of his apartments and houses. I did that for two years, and then he sold all his properties in the West Palm Beach area and moved to Port St. Lucie. He wanted me to join him, but I did not want to move. We are still friends today. He has a lovely lady friend named Jackie. Jackie has a daughter Olivia and her lovely grandmother Pat.

My friend Garth, Joy, and I.

The time came; I sold my second floor condominium and bought one on the first floor in Leisureville in Boynton Beach, Florida. I joined We-Care in Leisureville and by the Sea in Boca Raton, Florida.

Standing at the front door of my condominium in my Barber Shop Singers uniform.

In my travels for We-Care, I would pick up people and take them to the doctor or hospital. I have met many fine people. I was assigned to pick up a lady by the name of Laura. I arrived at her address and the garage door was open. When I walked halfway in, I saw her sitting on the cement floor. I asked her, "How long have you been sitting there?" She said she did not know. I lifted her up and inched her to my car. When I arrived at the doctor's office, I was able to get a wheelchair. The next day, I was able to get a wheelchair and potty for her, which We-Care provided. The potty was next to her bed. I took it upon myself to look after her. I found out that whenever I lifted her up with my left hand on her back, she would hurt. Then I asked her to put her arms around my neck. That was much better for her because it did not hurt so much. I made her breakfast, and then I told her that I needed to go home for a while and make some calls. I had no sooner arrived at home when she called me because she needed help. By the time I was able to get back to her it was 8:30 P.M. or 9:00 P.M. She was quite alert, so while I was gone, I had another woman sit with her to keep her company and bathe her. I also had another lady coming in to clean the house and make her chicken soup.

I asked her if I could tell her farm stories. She said, "No, but will you tell me about Christmas?" I started to tell her about Jesus' birth and that He grew up in a carpenter's home. As He grew up, He was found many times in the synagogue. He would chase out the moneychangers and said, "This is a house of prayer." Later, He fed 5,000 people. He did good things for all. There were bad people, and they did not like what Jesus had to say or do. So in time, they crucified Him. He died for you and me. She put her left hand on her chest and she repeated, "Jesus died for me." By that time, it was 10:30 P.M., and I was so happy that she laid her hand on her chest. The following day was the same. I was looking after her every day to take her to the doctor, and one evening she was alert again. It was approximately 9:00 P.M. or 10:00 P.M. I asked her if I could sing her a song, "I'm Working on the Railroad." I asked her if she would help me sing, and she said as sweet as she could be, "John, I forgot." I learned this song in 1950 when I immigrated to Ontario, Canada. My farmer boss drove me to a large school. A bilingual teacher gave up his time to teach us the song as well as the ABC's. She was still so awake. The other song I knew was "Jesus Loves Me." I sang this to her three or four times, and I saw her lips moving to the words that I was singing. Then she put her hand on her chest and said, "Jesus loves me." I felt like my mission was complete. Her daughter then came from Virginia to take care of her mother. At that point, I was only needed to drive them to the doctor. Laura passed on at the age of 95. May she rest in peace.

The American Cancer Society was looking for a driver to pick up cancer patients to drive them to different hospitals in our area. I was interviewed; they (six people) asked if I knew the area. I told them that I used to be an eighteen wheeler driver, and I knew the area well. The fifteen-passenger van I was hired to drive was donated by businesses in the area. I really enjoyed my job. For one thing I had to be on time, and I was 99.9% of the time. I saw all kinds of cancer patients; with some I could joke. One day I said that you are lucky that your laundry is being done every week. I told them that I do my laundry only once a month. They laughed; only once a month! I said, "I lay on one side one week, the second week I lay on the other side, the third week I lay along the feet section, the fourth week I lay across by the head section." We all could not stop laughing.

I worked for the American Cancer Society.

When I came to St. Mary's, I called my boss. She wanted to know how many people I had picked up and whom. One day I picked up everybody from their hospitals and brought them all to St. Mary's waiting room. I asked if they needed something; I had to wait for two of my patients to see their doctor. I went to sit on a nice chair. I had my eyes closed praying for my patient. Meantime my boss called and asked, "What is John doing?" The receptionist told my boss that I was sleeping. It was about 5:15 P.M. I walked around to check on my patients when it was 5:30 P.M. On the way home I got a call from my boss asking that I come to the office. She told me because I was sleeping on the job, I was fired. I told her that we all had to wait for our patients there at St. Mary's Hospital. No excuse.

At present, I worship at Lakeside Assembly of God on Old Boynton Beach Road in Boynton Beach, Florida. I enjoy the fellowship there.

This is my new pastor Joe and his lovely wife Nicky

3560 Old Boynton Road
Lakeside Christian Church of the Assembly of God, the church I attend.

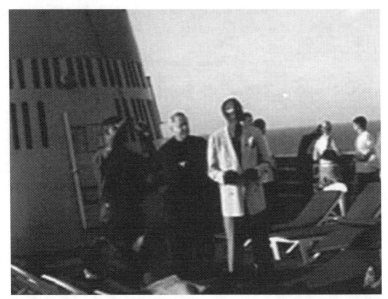

This is a church gathering on a dinner cruise. Pastor Miles is standing in the middle.

The Leisureville Barber Shop Singers.

I also joined the Barber Shop Singers in the area where I live in Leisureville. This group is made up of men from other parts of the United States and Canada. We get together when they are in Florida on winter vacation. The Barber Shop Singers sing in a church and club houses. The last two Christmases we practiced to sing Christmas songs. Three or four of us German men in the group sang "Silent Night," or in German, "Stille Nacht." Everyone there enjoyed the song. We also have hymn singing every Friday night. I cannot go all the time. When the snowbirds are here in the wintertime the clubhouse is full. They hold many different functions and dinners in Clubhouse Three.

The Hospice by the Sea office in Boca Raton assigned me to visit a fine Jewish man. Upon meeting him, he immediately told me that he was an atheist. All I could say was, "If you can live with it, that is all right with me." As time went by, we became friends. He asked me to pick him up to go out to eat on many occasions. He enjoyed when we went out for a drive. He lived in an apartment and had a housekeeper. As weeks went by, one day this kind man said, "When I die, we will see each other in heaven." I was surprised to have heard that from him. I asked him what changed his mind. His response was, "John, just the way you talk and behave and that you never talk about your faith." I told him, "The reason I never discussed my faith was because you told me that you are an atheist, and I was respecting your wishes." He was pleased with that. After a month or so, his daughter came to take care of him. I still went to visit him. She transferred him to a different location for hospice care and within a month, he died. The office I worked out of called to inform me that the patient that I had worked with had passed on. May he rest in peace.

One day, I was assigned to see a man in hospice care at his house. When I arrived, his wife had him in their bedroom in a hospital bed. I was there for about one hour. When I got back home, I was thinking of him. I called his wife and asked, "Could I come back to stay with you when your husband dies?" She asked, "Would you?" She gave me her second bedroom, and in the morning we had our breakfast at 7:30 A.M. We went to her husband at about 8:15 A.M., and he took his last breath. I was there in the eleventh hour. I stayed until the nurse and chaplain came. I felt my job was done. However I stayed in contact with the man's wife, Gisella. May he rest in peace.

One of my patients, by the name of Irvin, with his housekeeper.

I was visiting a patient of mine at her house one day and a lady chaplain came in. She prepared herself to give this lady her communion, and when it came time to pray the Lord's Prayer, the chaplain reached out for me to join in with them.

I am so glad that I am with Hospice by the Sea, and I encourage the patients to hang in there. I tell them not to fear death. God will be on your side, if they just ask Him. People ask me why I do hospice care. My answer is that when I experienced tragedy with my dear family, people were there for me. Now I want to give back what I have received in my times of need.

A lady that I have known for many years, Gloria, lives in Florida. I have also met her mom. One day Gloria came up with the idea to feed the hungry, as her mom would have liked her to do one day. She had things organized to go to the Westgate Church to feed the poor people. I was also in the serving line to feed them. At one point a little girl came up to me, after she had received a plate full of food. She asked, "Can I have more?" Her mouth, face, and hands were all greasy from the chicken thighs I dished out earlier. She was about five to seven years old. I felt so sorry for her. I met German girls just like her, when I could give 1 kg of flour to each person that came to me. My heart went out to them all. I remembered that during the war, I was one of those who begged for food. I could relate especially to this little girl; I know how it feels to be hungry. My stomach growled for food; I'm sure this little girl's stomach growled too. This is probably why she came back to me for more food. I wish I could have taken her home with me. I would have given her new clothes, and she would have had her own bed to sleep on. Later, after everything was done, I told Gloria that we should do this more often. During the war I was so hungry; if I could have, I would have eaten a wolf.

Gloria, my good friend, and I.

The second lady from the left is Gloria's mother. I had the honor of meeting her.

One day I forgot my glasses when I wanted to buy groceries. I went to buy cans of chunky chicken and brought them home. While I was eating, I thought the chicken tasted somewhat different. I put on my glasses and read the label. I found out that I had eaten dog food. I did not feel sick. That prompted me to have my glasses on the next time I bought canned food. I learned my lesson.

One day my niece Rosemary called and told me that her mom, my sister, Rose was in the hospital. I told her, "I will come to see you all." I was sad to hear that she had put one foot on a chair, lost her balance and fallen against the door frame. She fractured her back. I visited her as often as Rosemary could. I was there for two months. I spent Christmas with Rosemary and family, as well as with Pat and my son John.

My niece told me that it was not necessary for me to lease a car. I also had my son who would drive me to places whenever I wanted to go somewhere. Then I called the Walkers, who were good friends. They told me their son was coming to visit them. He is a Lutheran German minister. I've heard him preach in German two times. He took some of his time to drive me to his parents' house. I spent one to two days with them. On the way home, I wanted to see my farm. I saw the barn; the silo was gone. The house stood. A flood of happiness and joy filled my soul. I relived some of my earlier experiences. I saw my children playing. I also had a big sorrow; my wife couldn't help me anymore. I was way overloaded with work. In the main barn, I had purebred Holstein cattle, young and old. In the other barn I had sows. I kept the litters until big enough for slaughter.

Thinking back, I had a nice family. My wife Lena, daughter Cindy and son Karl are buried in the Brotherston Cemetery. My son's wife Debby and my granddaughter Karin are buried in the Elma Cemetery in Atwood. A flood of joy came over me about my dear family, and then a big sorrow filled my soul.

The Gellner family, my sister Rose's daughter Rosemary and her husband Andy along with their sons Jeffery and Christopher cared for me for two months while I was living there. I really appreciated their hospitality. I grew up in this kind of a tradition.

My third oldest sister, Rose.

The Gellner Family, my sister Rose's daughter Rosemary and husband Andy
with their sons. Jeffrey is on the right, and Christopher is on the left.
They are in our traditional dress.

This is my wife's sister Sophie to my left, two sons and one daughter with their spouses, and my son Johnny is on the left on the back row.

My wife's oldest sister's daughter, Katie, who is married to a man in Ottawa. He is in the middle of the picture. Their name is Rauch.

While I was in Canada for two months, my son drove me to Elmira where I visited my sister-in-law Sofie Plein, my wife's sister. I hadn't seen her for over 32 years. Sofie told me that her husband George Plein was buried in Elmira Cemetery. After the visit we went to the cemetery to see my brother-in-law's burial plot, and also the burial plot of Peter Both, who was a dairy farmer and friend of mine in the past. I met Peter because I saw in the farm section of the newspaper that another farmer had a boar hog for sale. After I saw the boar hog, we just drove across the highway to Peter's farm. This man wanted to introduce me to Peter because he was also a German. There I met him and his wife for the first time. Peter whispered in my ear in German not to buy the boar hog. Later on, Peter told me about the man's reputation. We visited each other often, and we even took vacations together to Boca Raton, Florida. When my wife passed away, Peter's wife came and selected a dress for my wife to wear for the burial.

My son drove me to Elmira to see my sister-in-law, my wife's sister, and on the way, I spotted this snowman. Here I am standing in front of the snowman.

Pat on the left, I in the middle, and my son Johnny on the right, in the Gellner's backyard.

My son Johnny and I in the Gellner's dining room.

Pat, the second from the left, with her three daughters, and I.

Later, after visiting the Walkers, the young minister's parents and their son Adam drove me to the farm and the gravestone. I put my hand on it. Again a flood of joy filled my soul to have had my dear wife for 28 years;

then the sorrow came. Although she had told me that she was going to die, I didn't take her seriously.

I knew she was a hard worker. We worked very well together. She was not afraid of anything. Sorrow over-flooded my soul that she left me to fend for myself. I was grateful that this young man, Adam, had his life's calling to be a Lutheran minister. He had to go to Germany to learn the German language. While he was there, I received his address from his mother. I wrote him a letter in English and another letter in German with the same content, just in case he didn't understand a word or sentence. He told me that he appreciated the letters that I had written to him while he was in Germany.

I knew the Walker's son, Adam, as a teenager. He is a German Lutheran minister. May the good Lord bless his ministry.

On a very sad note, on August 15, 2007, I received a call from my niece who informed me that her mom, my third oldest sister, had passed away. I told her that I would come. May my sister rest in peace. I was there for two weeks.

Another very sad day for me to see my dear sister Rose in there.

**The service at the graveside of my dear sister Rose.
She is being buried next to her dear husband, Martin Poschner.**

My niece, Rosemary, and her husband stand next to her mother's coffin.
It was a very sad day for us all.

My sister and her husband's gravestone.

This is the grave of my sister and her husband in Lutheran's Cemetery in Kitchener, Ontario, Canada.

The week following the funeral we were invited for a week at a cottage; we went and had a good time. The owner of the cottage was John Klein. His wife is the sister of my niece's husband Andy Gellner. I knew the Kleins' father and mother quite well. The Kleins also lived in my village.

This picture is at the Klein's cottage. John Klein is on the left, to the left of him his wife, hen Andy Gellner on the right, and I'm in the middle. I shall never forget the good times. Every day we played the card game UNO.

We had nice boat rides. I really enjoyed them. Behind me is John Klein.

My niece Rosemary and I at the cottage.

**One day my niece Rosemary and her husband Andy and
I went out to dinner at a restaurant.**

While I was in Canada, I came across a book that contained a lot of information about Transylvania. I read it with interest. I thought about the years of my life spent in that area and the happy times and difficult times for my family, me, and all the other people in that area.

With tears in my eyes, I saw on television the devastation the people in New Orleans had to endure because of Hurricane Katrina. Those people walked and sat in the water with no food, drinking water or shelter. My heart went out to them. I went through the same thing just without hurricane water. I lost my home and my country that I grew up in, loved, and was familiar with. Today I can say the United States is my country too. If we had not fled my country, we may have been taken to Siberian coal mines. The reason we left our country was because of the Russians. I was called a D.P., a displaced person. I met women in Canada that had been in Siberia. Where the military was, they had everyone under their control.

**This is a picture of the damage from Hurricane Wilma,
in our area here in South Florida.**

In my life in Canada and the United States, I have made many friends. Also, I have tried to help people and stay involved in activities such as hospice care and driving people to medical appointments. My family and friends and people I have just met have been so kind to me and have helped me in so many ways.

I really appreciate the help I received from different people to work on this book. There are too many people who helped me along the way to name them all. Then, I met a lovely lady named Donna, who was more than willing to help me get my book done. I had met her at Lakeside Christian Church, my home church in Boynton Beach, Florida. She had to go home to Philadelphia to help look after her uncle. I found a lovely lady named Debbie Barwick in the church who was willing to get this job done.

This is a lovely lady friend, Donna. She was tremendous in helping start and work on my story. Here she is holding her godson, Israel; she really loves this child. May God bless her mightily.

This is another lovely lady, Phillipa, who helped me with my memoir. We went on the Jungle Queen for a day cruise.

My lovely lady friend Debbie Barwick.

This lady lived upstairs, second floor in Leisureville Building D.
I live in Building C. I drove her often to the doctor and places she needed to go.
She is a lovely lady at 103 years old.

Mr. and Mrs. Bob Zimmerman, another fine couple I met in Leisureville.

This lovely lady, named Marie, sold me this car; she practically gave it to me. May God bless her for her generosity. She told me that because of my volunteering with Hospice By the Sea and We-Care, I needed a better car.

Through all the struggles that I have faced in my life, I never lost my faith. My continued strength comes from the Bible verses in Romans 8 verses 35-39 that says, "Who shall separate us from the love of Christ? Shall trouble or hardship or persecution or famine or nakedness or danger or sword? As it is written: 'For Your sake we face death all day long; we are considered as sheep to be slaughtered.' Know in all these things we are more than conquerors through Him who loved us. For I am convinced that neither death nor life, neither angels nor demons, neither the present nor the future nor any powers, neither height nor depth, nor anything else in all creation will be able to separate us from the love of God that is in Christ Jesus our Lord." Amen!